PAUL ARCHER

CeMAP 2
REVISION GUIDE

CeMAP© 2

Revision Guide 2019/2020

Paul Archer

High House Publishing

© Archer Training Ltd 2000 - 2019

This book is copyright under the Berne Convention.

No reproduction without permission.

All rights reserved. The right of Paul Archer to be identified as the author of this work has been asserted by him in accordance with sections 77 and 78 of the copyright designs and patents act, 1988. All rights reserved.

No part of this publication may be reproduced, stored in a retrieval system, or transmitted in any form, or by any means, electronic, mechanical, photocopying, recording and or otherwise without the proper permission of the publishers.

This book may not be lent, resold, hired out or otherwise disposed of by way of trade in any form, binding or Cover other than that in which it is published, without the prior consent of the publishers.

The Revision Guide, as with all our supporting material, is complementary to the main textbook and will never replace the detail contained therein. It was never written to reproduce the same text - that would serve no purpose. It does contain, however, bulleted summaries of the syllabus. These bullets are lighter in substance but retain the major points.

It is, essentially, a Revision Guide.

CeMAP® is a registered trademark of the London Institute of Banking and Finance. Use by Paul Archer of these marks does not imply any endorsement of our training material and courses by the LIBF.

First published in Great Britain in 2012 by High House Publishing, PO Box 1301, Cheltenham, GL50 9BQ, United Kingdom.

Seventeenth Edition

Printed and bound in Great Britain by Lulu.com

Edited by Lynnette Carter

Cover designed by Felicia Cornish

ISBN 978-0-9571738-5-9 (Paperback)

ISBN 978-0-9571738-4-2 (eBook)

For all your mortgage sales training needs, in house requirements contact Paul at

www.archertraining.com

www.paularcher.com

paul@paularcher.com

The Revision Guide's Contents

1 Mortgage Law, Policy, Practice & Markets	9
Personal borrowers	9
Semi Corporate Lending	10
Corporate Lending	11
Executors and trustees	12
Power of Attorney	13
Guarantors and Sureties	15
Voluntary Housing Sector	16
Ineligible Borrowers	17
Insolvency	18
Mortgage Regulation	20
MCOBs	23
Mortgage Market Review	31
Definitions of a mortgage	32
Legal Types of Mortgage	33
How Lenders Fund Lending	34
Types of Joint Ownership	36
Freehold	37
Leasehold	38
Commonhold	39
The Commonhold Enigma	40
Leaseholders' statutory rights	41
Covenants	42
Easements	43
Land Registration	44
Unregistered Land	46
Agricultural Holdings	50
Guaranteeing Title	51
Matrimonial Law	52
Chancel Repair Liability	53
Stamp Duty Land Tax (SDLT)	54
Conveyancing	56
Estate agents	58
Auctions	59
House Purchase Process	60
Common Property Defects	61
Property Terminology	67
The UK Mortgage Market	68
The Mortgage Players	70
Consumer Credit Acts	72
Consumer Insurance Act 2012	75
Agency Law	76
Contract Law	77
Energy Performance Certificates	78
The Consumer Protection (Amendment) Regulations 2014	79

2 Application for a Mortgage 80

Assessing the Income 80
Proving the Income 81
Credit Assessment 82
Advised Sales Rule Changes 83
Mortgage Disclosure 84
County Court Judgments 85
Fraud and Fraud Act 2006 86
Money Laundering 87
Buying and Selling Costs 88
Search Changes at the Local Level 89
CON29M – Mining Searches 90
Assessing the Property 91
The Survey Results 93
Factors Affecting Property Value 94
Property Value 95
Planning consent 102
Building Regulations 110
Listed Buildings 111
Higher Lending Charges 112
Other Security 113
Offer of Advance 114
Mortgage Deeds 116
The Mortgage Deed Lender's Rights 117
Property Insurance 118
Block Policies 119
Artificial Intelligence and Mortgage Advising 120

3 Mortgage Payment Methods & Products 123

Capital and interest mortgages 123
Interest-only mortgages 124
With Profit Endowments 126
Unit-linked Endowments 127
Endowment Shortfalls 129
Individual Savings Accounts ISAs 130
Personal Pension Plans 134
Term Assurance Policies 137
Variable Rate Mortgages 139
Base Rate Tracker Mortgages 140
Fixed Rate Mortgages 140
Capped Mortgages 141
LIBOR-related mortgages 141
Cashback Incentive 142
Guarantor Mortgages 143
Right to Buy Mortgages 144
Self-build Mortgages 145
Flexible Mortgages 146
Off-Set Mortgage 146
Buy To Let Mortgages 147
Why SPVs are OK 149
Deferred Mortgages 150
Sharia or Islamic Mortgages 151
Sub Prime and Non-Status Mortgages 152

HomeBuy Schemes	153
Help to Buy	154
Shared Ownership Mortgage	156
Foreign Currency Mortgages	157
100% Mortgages	158
Commercial Mortgages	159
Releasing Equity	160
Mortgage Payment Protection Insurance (MPPI)	163
Income Protection Insurance	164
ASU 2 - IPI 3	165
Critical Illness Cover	166
Annual Percentage Rate (APR)	167
Annual Percentage Rate of Charge (APRC)	168
Interest Rate Volatility	169
Interest Rests	170
Mortgage Products Summary	171
A Repayment Vehicle MOT	183

4   Post Completion 184

Further advances	184
Lender Assistance with Arrears	187
Arrangements	188
Government Support for Arrears and Repossessions	189
Taking Possession	190
Selling a Repossessed Property	191
Alternative Remedies	192
Repossession Register	193
How is the Debt Chased?	194
Transfers of equity	195
Transfers of Equity and SDLT	196
Early redemption	197
Redemption	198
Transferring the Mortgage Book	199
Lettings of mortgaged property	200
Unauthorised Tenancy	201
Release of part security	202
Death of a borrower	203
Bridging finance	205
Remortgaging	206
Secured Second mortgages	207
House Insurance Claims	208

5   CeMAP 2 Specimen Exam 209

Answers	232

1 Mortgage Law, Policy, Practice & Markets

Personal borrowers

- Majority of borrowers for mortgage loans and comprise of first-time buyers and subsequent buyers.

- Income multiples were often used where salaries and additional incomes are multiplied by set amounts to give a maximum loan. Often regular outgoings such as personal loan payment are deducted from salary before applying the multiple.

- Affordability where lenders ensure that the applicant's income and expenditure is examined before deciding how much they can borrow.

- Under the Mortgage Market Review, the regulator has imposed more rigorous requirements on checking affordability.

- Mortgages can be arranged in joint names, but payments are required from all borrowers – they are not split like property ownership. This is known as a joint and several liability.

Semi Corporate Lending

- To a business where there is a residential element, e.g. corner shop with flat above or the picture below which shows a garage with accommodation above.
- This is also known as commercial lending as the borrower is a commercial borrower.

Corporate Lending

- To a limited company or body with a separate legal identity.
- Higher risk than residential lending, therefore, may be higher interest rates and shorter terms.
- Is not regulated under the FCA.

Factors when lending to a limited company

- Is the person promoting the advance acting on behalf of the company?
- Is the company a close company?
- Shares owned by an individual or a family.
- Does the company's memorandum permit it to borrow?
- It is demonstrated by a minute of a formal meeting.
- Is the company a good credit risk?
- Three-year assessment of performance?
- Building Societies cannot hold more than 25% of assets in loans to limited companies secured on land.

Guarantors

- Lenders may require when lending to a company, that the directors personally become guarantors.
- This is to ensure that if the company (a separate legal entity) defaults, the owners of the company can be pursued for the money.

Executors and trustees

Personal representatives

- Act in managing the estates of deceased persons. They are:
  - Executors if named in a will.
  - Administrator if appointed by Letters of Administration (no will).
- Lenders can lend to personal representatives if the loan is for administering the estate.

Trustees

- Have the responsibility of dealing with trust property, by the terms of a trust deed, in the interests of the beneficiaries.
- If the trust deed contains the power to create a mortgage, a lender may be prepared to make a loan.

Power of Attorney

- It's worth noting LPAs replaced the previous Enduring Power of Attorney (EPA) system. EPAs set up before 1 October 2007 will still be valid, whether or not they have been registered, though they must be registered when the person loses capacity. For more, see the Government's EPA info.

The Health and Welfare Lasting Power of Attorney

- In a nutshell, the health and welfare document sees a nominated individual make decisions over day-to-day healthcare and medical treatments, as well as deal with any health and social care staff. It's also worth noting these are two separate legal procedures that are independent of one another.

- Just because you give the trusted person power of attorney over your health, that doesn't mean they will automatically gain control over your financial affairs and vice versa. If you require the same individual to have power of attorney over both aspects of your care, then you will have to fill out the two forms separately.

- Another key difference is that the health and welfare LPA can only be used after the person loses capacity, not before. For more help on setting up a health and welfare LPA, see the Government's health & welfare LPA info. For those who want to decide any 'advance decisions' – e.g., you don't want certain types of medical treatment in certain situations, if you lose capacity in future – you can make a living will.

Power of Attorney Cost

- There's a compulsory cost of £82 to register a Power of Attorney (in England and Wales – it's £77 in Scotland, £127 in Northern Ireland). If you earn less than £12,000/year though, you can provide evidence to have a reduced fee of £41. Those on certain benefits are exempt from fees.

- It's £82 each for the property and finance LPA and the health and welfare LPA, so if you get both, that's £164.

- Above and beyond that, if you decide to use a solicitor, you'll also have to pay legal fees, though it's

Why Set Up a Lasting Power of Attorney?

- If you lose mental capacity, unless you've already filled in the Power of Attorney forms, your loved ones will need to apply through court to become 'deputy', a long and expensive process.

- Instead, you can nominate a trusted friend or relative before you lose capacity, by setting up a Lasting Power of Attorney (LPA). You can appoint one or more representatives to act for you and can determine how they work together to make decisions on your behalf.

- You may be thinking "this doesn't affect us, we're perfectly well". This is a common misunderstanding.

- You can only set up a Lasting Power of Attorney when you have mental capacity. Once you've lost capacity, it's too late.

- In Scotland, there are three Powers of Attorney: one for financial matters, called a continuing Power of Attorney; one for personal welfare, a welfare Power of Attorney; and a combined POA that covers both continuing and welfare, which is the most common.

- When you make a Power of Attorney in England and Wales, a 'certificate provider' decides if you're capable of making that choice. This can be someone you've known for two years or someone with relevant professional skills such as a doctor, lawyer or social worker.

Application

- This is the best time to act. If the person still has capacity and would like to make arrangements in case they lose mental capacity, they can set up a Lasting Power of Attorney.

- Once submitted, it takes up to ten weeks to register. The power will be effective as soon as the LPA is registered so the attorney will be able to start making decisions straight away unless they specify otherwise on the application.

  - Step 1. Decide whether to use a solicitor
  - Step 2. Doing it yourself? Make your application via an online form
  - Step 3. Register the Power of Attorney

Guarantors and Sureties

- A guarantor is someone who makes a legally enforceable contractual commitment to be responsible for paying back the loan if a principal borrower defaults.

- A surety is a guarantor who puts up something of value as collateral.

- Lenders call their newest products "Guarantee Mortgages" and these use guarantors to reduce the risk for the lender.

"I would probably do better in school if I had a pony."

Voluntary Housing Sector

- Registered Social Landlords (RSLs) often referred as housing associations, which are non-profit-making organisations that provide housing for rental or purchase.
- The Housing and Regeneration Act 2008 abolished the Housing Corporation, which until that time had been responsible for Registered Social Landlords and created two new bodies.
  - The Homes and Communities Agency.
  - The Tenant Services Authority.
- The Act created a new term 'registered providers'.
- Many financial institutions are prepared to make long-term funds available to well-run associations.

Homes and Communities Agency HCA

- Provides affordable housing in developing communities
- Sponsored by government and local government
- The Localism Act 2011 covers issues surrounding proving local housing
- Being a Registered Provider enables organisations to get grants to develop areas

Clubs and Associations

- Clubs and associations are able to borrow only if their rules and terms of reference allow.
- Managed by committees on behalf of their members.

Ineligible Borrowers

Mental incapacity

- Persons of unsound mind cannot borrow in their own right.
- A person of unsound mind cannot make a power of attorney.
- If such a person requires housing to be funded by a mortgage, a person appointed by the Court of Protection represents them.

Minors

- Persons under 18 years of age.
- Law of Property Act 1925: a minor cannot hold an interest in land.
- Minor's Contracts Act 1987: a minor cannot be bound by a contract unless it is for "necessities".
- Mortgages are not available to persons under 18.
- Consumer Credit Act 1974 – a minor cannot enter into an agreement regulated by this Act - if they do the contract is unenforceable.

Insolvency

- Insolvency occurs when
  - A person's liabilities exceed his assets; or
  - A person cannot meet his financial obligations when they fall due.
  - Insolvency arises when an order is made under the Insolvency Act 1986.

Bankruptcy

- A person's liabilities exceed his assets;
- A person cannot meet his financial obligations within a reasonable period of their falling due.
- The order usually remains in force for 1 year under the Enterprise Act 2002.
- During this time:
  - The person is an un-discharged bankrupt.
  - He cannot borrow more than nominal amounts.
- After that time
  - He can borrow if a lender is prepared to lend.
  - Earlier bankruptcy must be declared.

Individual voluntary arrangements (IVAs)

- An IVA is an alternative to bankruptcy.
- The debtor arranges with creditors to reschedule outstanding debts over a certain period.
- Creditors with at least 75% of the debts must agree to the arrangement.
- Persons subject to IVAs are a poor credit risk
- Although there is nothing legally to prevent an individual who is in an IVA from borrowing.

Mortgage Law, Policy, Practice & Markets

Debt Relief Orders

- Brought in as a result of legislation, DROs allow people in debt to receive years grace and then for the loans to be wiped out. These people will have their credit record tarnished for many years to come.
- People need to be struggling with debt, have limited disposable income and no assets
- After a year of the lenders not being able to enforce payments, so long as they have kept to the conditions, the debts are written off.
- The Insolvency Service and approved advisers can arrange DROs
- Conditions to apply are:
  - Domiciled in England and Wales
  - Owe £20,000 maximum
  - Their assets must not exceed £1,000
  - Have a disposable income of no more than £50
  - Not have applied for bankruptcy or a DRO in the previous 6 years

Mortgage Regulation

- Few people can believe it, but the advice and running of a residential mortgage was unregulated 15 years ago. In 2004 they became regulated, the FCA provides rules and guidance on how these are sold and run. MCOBs rule the waves but not for every mortgage.

- Mortgages sold to individuals are regulated as are loans to finance a property where more than 40% of the property is being used as the main dwelling. You may hear the word MCD – Mortgage Credit Directive – which came In during 2016 and tightened up the rules of mortgage lending and admin. Most mortgages today are effectively MCD regulated because they adhere to these new rules.

- MCD was renowned for bringing second charge loans into regulation. These are loans secured on property where the owner already has a first mortgage on it. They are generally more expensive but readily available compared to first loans.

- Loans not in the team are "buy to lets" unless they are being granted to a consumer who didn't want to let the property, but have to because of the situation. These are known as consumer buy to lets. Professional Landlords who take our buy to let mortgages are not regulated, the definitions are strict but usually stipulate 4 or more houses to be owned or a landlord that wants to become a full-time landlord, not someone who just stumbled across a buy to let need.

- Corporate loans are excluded and well outside the CeMAP syllabus.

- Lifetime mortgages are in the club of regulated loans, and rightly so. Thes loans occupy the later life lending market and include home reversion plans which are not loans at all but regulated as such. Separate MCOB rules must be adhered to for lifetime mortgages and home reversion plans. Smart regulations to protect the consumer, and keep them in their home until death or moving into a care home.

- The newest member of the later life market is RIOs – retirement interest-only mortgages – these are regulated but are sold by standard mortgage advisers – you need special permission and exams to advise in the later life market. RIOs are interest-only mortgages with no end date – they are repaid on death.

- Home purchase plans, also known as Islamic Finance, are also regulated. To appreciate these products, an understanding of Sharia or Islamic Law is needed. Thou shall not receive or pay interest is the mantra, and a traditional mortgage falls foul of this since interest is both paid and received by the bank.

- Islamic loans involve the bank buying the property and then "leasing" it back to the owner by 25 years or so of instalments. Of course, it achieves the same aim but doesn't involve interest.

Buy to Let Mortgages

- Previously Buy to Let mortgages were not regulated by the FCA since they fall outside of the 40% rule and are generally not lived in by family members.

- This has now changed with the FCA preferring to distinguish between:
    - Buy to Let mortgages arranged by a business and
    - Buy to Let mortgage arranged by an individual or consumer

- They're regulating the one arranged by a consumer but not the one organised by a business. The vast majority of professional landlords who use Buy to Let mortgages to build up their property portfolios, do so via a company of some sort to minimise taxation.

- The FCA recognises that some people inherit a buy to let mortgage with a let to buy, where their existing home is rented out on a temporary basis whilst they live elsewhere. These people need protection, and the mortgage needs to be regulated. Providers of these will have to adhere to the MCOBs from now on.

Second Charge Lending

- In a similar manner to Buy to Lets, 2nd Charge Lending is now under the guidance of the FCA and providers must adhere to the MCOBs.

- And rightly so. They are dealing with consumers, often arranging large sums on the security of residential homes. They offer slightly easier lending terms with the ubiquitous higher interest rates.

- So rather than be regulated by the new CONC, which provide the rules for firms involved in the consumer credit market, providers are pretty much on par with first charge mortgage lenders.

Unfair Practices

- Mortgage cold call selling will not be allowed.
- Excessive fees will not be permitted.
- Key Facts Illustrations must illustrate fees.
- All mortgage arrangement fees must be included in APR.

Training & Competence

- Advisers must adhere to the normal T&C requirements unless already competent.
- Additional training required for lifetime mortgages.

Complaints and Compensation

- Lenders and intermediaries fall under Financial Ombudsman Service and Compensation Scheme.

MCOBs

MCOB 1: Application and purpose

- Explains the scope of the rules, i.e. to whom they apply and for what types of mortgage.

MCOB 2: Conduct of business standards

- Includes:
    - the use of correct terminology ('early repayment charge' and 'higher lending charge');
    - the requirement for communications with customers to be 'clear, fair and not misleading';
    - rules about the payment of fees / commission and the accessibility of records for inspection by the FCA.

MCOB 2A: Mortgage Credit Directive:

- Includes rules on a range of matters that apply to a lender classed as a Mortgage Credit Directive mortgage lender, including:
    - remuneration;
    - the tying of products (making a mortgage conditional on the purchase of other products);
    - foreign currency loans; and early repayments.

MCOB 3A: Financial promotions

- Distinguishes between 'real-time' promotions (by personal visit or telephone call) and non-real-time (by letter, email, or advert in newspapers, magazines, or on television radio or the internet).

  - Unsolicited real-time promotions are not permitted.

  - Non-real-time promotions must include the name and contact details of the firm. They must be clear, fair and not misleading. If comparisons are used, they must be with products that meet the same needs.

  - They must state that 'your home may be repossessed if you do not keep up repayments on your mortgage'. Records of non-real-time promotions must be retained for one year after their last use.

MCOB 3B: MCD general information

- Specifies the requirements relating to information that must be provided to customers, for lenders who make mortgage advances regulated under the Mortgage Credit Directive.

MCOB 4 and 4A: Advising and selling standards

- It must be clear whether advice is based on the products of the whole market, a limited number of home finance providers, or a single lender.

    - Independent advisers are not required to be able to access all products from all providers: they can source products from a panel of lenders as long as the panel is representative of the market.

    - Any mortgage recommended must be suitable for the customer and appropriate to their needs and circumstances; records to demonstrate this must be kept for three years. However, there is no requirement to issue a suitability report to the client.

    - Special requirements apply if the mortgage will be used to consolidate existing debts.

- On first making contact with a customer, certain information must be disclosed prominently and clearly to the customer. An initial disclosure document (IDD) can be given to detail the required information, but this is not a formal requirement as long as the required information is clearly communicated. The customer must be provided with the following information:

    - name and contact details;

    - whose mortgages are offered;

    - details of any limitations in service;

    - details of any fee payable for the mortgage advice;

    - the firm's FCA registration details;

    - how to complain; and

    - details of the compensation scheme.

MCOB 5 and 5A: Pre-application disclosure

- Details the information that must be provided at the point at which a personal recommendation is made and before an application is submitted to the lender. This must include:

  - the annual percentage rate of charge (APRC), which shows the interest rate with any fees added;

  - the amount of the monthly instalment; and

  - the amount by which the instalment would increase for each 1 per cent rise in interest rates

MCOB 6 and 6A: Disclosure at the offer stage

- If a mortgage offer is made, the lender must provide a detailed offer document. This is based on the information given at pre-application stage, subject to any changes between application and offer illustration. The offer is binding on the lender but can be made conditional on the confirmation of certain details. The offer must also:

  - state how long the offer will remain valid;

  - point out that there will be no right of withdrawal after the mortgage has been completed; and

  - include or be accompanied by a tariff of charges.

- The borrower must be granted a period of reflection of at least seven days to consider whether to accept the offer or not.

MCOB 7 and 7A: Disclosure at start of contract and after sale

- Before the first mortgage payment is made, the lender must confirm:

  ➢ details of amounts, dates and methods of payment;

  ➢ details of any related products such as insurance;

  ➢ (for interest-only mortgages) the responsibility of the borrower to ensure that a repayment vehicle is in place; and what the customer should do if they fall into arrears.

- Annual statements must be issued, showing:

  ➢ the amount owed and remaining term;

  ➢ what type of mortgage it is;

  ➢ for interest-only mortgages, a reminder to check the performance of the repayment vehicle;

  ➢ interest, fees or other payments made since the last statement;

  ➢ any changes to the charges tariff since the last statement

- If the mortgage is arranged on an interest-only basis, then the lender must contact the borrower at least once during the term to confirm that a credible repayment vehicle remains in place.

- If a change is to be made to the monthly payment, the customer must be informed of the new amount, revised interest rate and date of the change.

MCOB 8 and 9: Equity release

- Details the FCA's requirements in respect of lifetime mortgages and home reversion schemes. Special rules apply to equity release in relation to advising and selling standards, and to product disclosure.

- The FCA Training and Competence rules require that anyone giving advice on equity release must hold a specialist qualification in this area of business.

MCOB 10: Annual percentage rate (APR)

- Describes how to calculate APR

MCOB 10A: Annual percentage rate of charge

- Describes how to calculate APRC

MCOB 11 and 11A: Responsible Lending

- Lenders must put in place a written responsible lending policy and must be able to show that they have taken into consideration a customer's ability to pay when offering a mortgage.

MCOB 12: Charges

- Excessive charges are not permitted. Early repayment charges must be a reasonable approximation of the costs incurred by the lender if the borrower repays the full amount early.

- Similarly, arrears charges must be a reasonable approximation of the cost of additional administration as the result of a borrower being in arrears.

MCOB 13: Arrears and repossessions

- Firms must deal fairly with customers who have mortgage arrears or mortgage shortfall debt. This includes:

  - trying to reach an agreement on how to repay the arrears, taking into account the borrower's circumstances;

  - liaising with third-party sources of advice;

  - not putting unreasonable pressure on customers in arrears;

  - repossessing a property only when all other reasonable measures have failed;

  - only applying arrears charges that are a reasonable reflection of the costs of the work involved in dealing with the arrears.

- Records must be kept of all dealings with borrowers in arrears.

- Customers in arrears must be given the following information within 15 working days of the lender becoming aware of arrears:

  - Information sheet 'Problems paying your mortgage';

  - the missed payments and the total of arrears including any charges incurred;

  - the outstanding debt;

  - any further charges that may be incurred unless arrears are cleared.

MCOB 14 – Rules and guidance for MCD

- Applies rules and guidance in MCOB
- Covers loans taken by individuals and trustees.
- The property must be in the EEA and be at least 40% lived in by the borrower or family.
- Rules cover most aspects – lending, administration, and advice.
- All lenders and intermediaries need authorisation.
- Mortgage sales must occur on an advisory basis or in certain cases execution-only basis.
- Advice requirements ensure that:
  - The customer can afford the loan, now and in the future.
  - That a mortgage is indeed suitable.
  - The most suitable type of mortgage and mortgage product is selected.
  - The most suitable lender is chosen.
- Home Reversion Plans.
  - Although not strictly mortgages as a 3rd party buys a share of someone's property in return for a lump sum or income.
  - Since April 2007, these are now regulated by the FCA.
- Home Finance Plans (HFPs).
  - Also known as Islamic or Sharia mortgages.
  - Since April 2007, these are also regulated.
- Lifetime Mortgages.
  - Available to borrowers of a certain age.
  - Full repayment sought when borrower dies, moves or sells.
  - No payments made although interests charged.
  - Also known as Roll Up Loans.

Mortgage Market Review

- The first major change in the mortgage since 2005 brought upon by the Credit Crunch and the main blame being laid against irresponsible lending.

- The main points are:
    - Income will have to be verified in every mortgage application – bringing an end to both self-certification and to fast-track mortgage products.
    - The rules for determining disposable income, to support affordability, are less prescriptive than originally proposed, but guidance on what lenders should consider is provided.
    - Lenders will have to decide on the "stress test" they wish to apply, to check that mortgage applicants will be able to afford the payments should interest rates rise.
    - Interest-only mortgages will still be permitted, but lenders will have to satisfy themselves that the borrower has a credible strategy to repay the capital at the end of the term.
    - The vast majority of sales will have to be carried out on an advised basis – all sales where there is human interaction, face to face, phone or email, will have to be advised. Only internet and postal "execution only" business for "high net worth and professional consumers" will be permitted.
    - Certain mortgage applicants who pose a higher risk to themselves, such as those consolidating debts, will have to get explicit advice.
    - And there will be special transitional rules for borrowers caught by changes in rules – the so-called "mortgage prisoners" – and both their existing lender or a new lender can apply transitional rules to ensure they're not disadvantaged if they wish to move home or remortgage.

Definitions of a mortgage

- Many people think the mortgage is the loan, but it is merely the security for the loan.

- It is a legal contract that enables a borrower to offer a property as security for a loan, thus enabling ownership of the property to be acquired.

- The mortgage is the Legal Charge, or Mortgage Deed agreed between the two parties, the lender and the borrower. The Mortgage is the security for the loan and gives the lender powers over the property whilst the loan is outstanding.

- The two parties to a mortgage are:
    - The borrower, known as the mortgagor.
    - The lender, known as the mortgagee.

- Now say the word mortgagor and really accentuate the "or" and immediately say borrower and emphasize the "er" and pronounce it "or". Repeat twice, and you won't forget the difference.

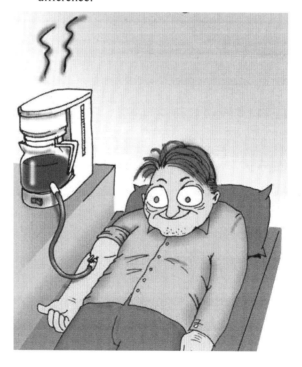

Legal Types of Mortgage

Mortgage by legal charge

- The most common form of mortgage in the UK.
- The purchaser owns the property, but the lender has a right over the land until the loan is fully repaid.
- The property is transferred by conveyance

Mortgage by demise

- Used prior to 1925. Property is owned by the lender when loan taken out.
- Property transferred from lender to borrower when loan is fully repaid, i.e. the loan has died.
- Abolished in the Land Registration Act 2002 for new mortgages with registered land.

Second and subsequent mortgages

- The borrower offers a property as security for an additional loan while another lender still has a mortgage on that property.
- That first mortgage is secured by a first charge on the property and the second loan is secured by a second charge.
- If a borrower defaults and the first lender sells the security, any surplus after their loan has been repaid must be passed to the second lender, and so on.

How Lenders Fund Lending

- When I first started in the mortgage industry, in 1982, the only funding for mortgage lending was the retail deposits provided by members of building societies. We had quotas or limits on how much we could lend strictly geared towards the inflow of saver's money. People used to walk into my office on their knees, begging for a mortgage.

- How times have changed.

- There is no shortage of money available to the UK mortgage market, which has created hundreds of mainstream and specialised lenders. They fund their mortgages via:

Retail Funding

- Much the way of the building society in 1982 and this model hasn't changed a bit. Lenders need a banking license to collect deposits and use interest rates and product features to lure in savings. You will recall the phrase "lending long", and this model allows for short term deposits to be used to fund long term mortgages.

- Margins are maintained to provide the profit. Paying interest at 1% and earning rates of 3% offers a 2% profit. This is eaten into with costs of marketing and such, but it is a robust model.

Securitisation

- Famed for causing the financial crash in 2008, mortgage-backed securities (MBS) allow lenders to move tranches of loans to other institutions without selling them off ultimately. The loans are still owned by the lender, and they receive repayments and deal with arrears and other matters.

- A small proportion of the monthly mortgage payments are paid to the holders of the MBS who provide a lump sum up front in return. Their lump sum is gradually repaid by the mortgage payments over a 20 to 25 year period. The lender is now armed with a large lump sum again which they can then re-lend.

Wholesale Market

- This is where lenders who don't have the retail deposits available, secure their funding for the short term before they embark on securitisation. It's a wide and varied marketplace, virtually a forum for institutions (banks, governments, corporates and the like) who have surplus cash, to lend it to those who need it to fund their mortgage operations.

- The standard approach is to seek warehouse lines of credit. These are repaid within two to three years — enough time to get lending and securitising to repay the loan. Often in the sum of £300 to £500 million and the providers will want some say in how the money is lent, this will impact on criteria.

- Peer to Peer lender, Lendinvest, has reported having received a £200 million line from HSBC, which it will use to finance its bridging loan activities. Interestingly it will use its Peer to Peer platform to attract investors to ultimately repay HSBC rather than securitise the whole lot in two or so years.

- Forward Flow Agreements, popular in the States, are methods of raising finance differently. One institution lends a large tranche of money to another. They lend this money on mortgage using the original lender's appetite to risk. Ultimately the loans are then transferred back to the original institution to sit on their balance sheet, and the whole process continues.

- With the world awash with cash seeking higher interest rate returns, with a minimum of risk, the supply of funding for the mortgage market seems endless. All it takes, though, is for confidence in the wholesale market to run out and funds will dry up overnight, causing a systemic crash.

- That's what happened in 2007 when Northern Rock Bank ran out of money and went to the wholesale market. There was no one at home that day; they'd all been frightened away. The rest is history.

Types of Joint Ownership

Joint tenancy

- Two or more people own an asset, i.e. a property, jointly and severally.
- On death, the whole asset belongs to the survivor and none of it to the beneficiaries of the estate of the deceased.
- Typically arranged for property ownership by married couples.

Tenancy in common

- An asset is held on a split basis, usually - but not necessarily - in equal shares.
- On the death of one party, their share of an asset held on this basis passes to their estate, not to the surviving person(s).
- Tenants in Common ownership tends to be for unmarried couples such as brothers buying together.

Joint borrowers

- There is no limit to the number of signatories on a mortgage.
- However, in practice, most lenders allow up to four.
- Almost all mortgages are established on a jointly and severally liable basis. This means that everyone is liable for the whole mortgage.

Freehold

- Freehold, leasehold and commonhold are the only types of land tenure in England and Wales at present. The Law of Property Act 1925 abolished all others.
- Freehold is the nearest you can get to absolute ownership.
- The crown has the overriding right to all property in its domain.
- The freeholder effectively owns the land; there may be many restrictions on what he can do with it, e.g.
  - The title may contain restrictions.
  - The local authority may impose restrictions on use or alterations.
  - Town and country planning legislation will apply.
  - Utilities (water, electricity, etc.) may have statutory rights.
  - There are obligations to people who enter the premises.
  - There are obligations to people who pass the building.
- Flying freehold is where part of someone's freehold property hangs over someone else's land.

Leasehold

- A freeholder effectively rents out land that he owns, for a fixed period, to others who then have the use of the land, subject to the payment of an annual ground rent, for as long as the lease remains operative.
- A crackdown on unfair leasehold practices was announced in 2018 with new measures to cut out unfair and abusive practices relating to ground rent within the leasehold system, including a ban on leaseholds for almost all new build houses.
- At the end of the lease, the land and any property on it revert totally to the freeholder.
- The leaseholder is bound by the same restrictions as might affect the freeholder if he had not leased the property. In addition, the freeholder may himself impose other conditions, e.g.:
  - Obligations as to repairs and maintenance;
  - Constraints on the use of the property;
  - Restrictions on alterations;
  - Duties in respect of any common areas (e.g. stairs in a block of flats).
- Lenders are interested in the terms of a lease, as a restrictive lease may reduce the resale value of a property.
- Unexpired term.
  - The time remaining until the end of the lease is very important since the land will then revert to the freeholder.
  - The value will fall as the lease approaches expiry date.
  - Lenders typically require there to be 30 - 40 years remaining on the lease.

Forfeiture

- Failure to comply with the terms of a lease can result in the lease being terminated, with the property reverting to the freeholder.
- This would be a problem for a lender, whose security would become worthless.
- Lenders, therefore, insist on a clause permitting them to fulfil the terms of a lease if the borrower fails to do so.
- Lenders can insure against the effects of forfeiture.

Commonhold

- The Commonhold and Leasehold Reform Act 2002 introduced a new form of tenure called Commonhold.

- Commonhold will be available for new developments, and the Act contains provisions which will allow conversion to Commonhold.

- Commonhold is a new form of Freehold ownership which has the flexibility of Leasehold so far as the division of the property is concerned. In a block of flats, the individual flats may be Commonhold, which is a freehold title and not leasehold for a term of years. The flats will therefore not start to devalue towards the end of their leases.

- Where a development is to be Commonhold, the flat owners will own their units as Common holders. The common parts of the block (roads, stairs, lobbies etc.) will be owned by the Commonhold Association which will be a company limited by guarantee. The members will be the individual unitholders on the development.

- The Commonhold Association will be responsible for the running of the development and the raising of service charges (called Commonhold Assessments).

- The development can be mixed-use and could consist of both houses and flats.

"THAT'S NOT RISING DAMP. IT'S BEEN THAT HIGH FOR YEARS."

The Commonhold Enigma

- The Commonhold method of owning a flat began in 2004, which much fanfare as it was intended to revolutionise the way flats were sold.

- However, it has gone down like a dam squid since only 20 developments have occurred in 14 years. So much so that the Law Commission is keen to know why.

- On the face of it, Commonhold is a no brainer for the buyer but not so for the developer, and that's the problem.

- Commonhold is far superior to owning as leasehold. Firstly it removed any lingering years of ownership and the worry of an every decreasing term of lease. It also gives each owner a say in how things are run and who is brought in to paint the walls in the form of a management company that runs the upkeep of the building. Plus, there's no need to pay a Ground Rent as there is no leaseholder.

- This is where Commonhold came unstuck. They removed a handy little cash cow that developers had. By creating leasehold homes, developers were able to sell the freehold on to funds who enjoyed the annual ground rent payments, often doubling every five or so years, a canny investment. Developers made quite a profit from this venture.

- Hopefully, the Law Commission, which is seeking opinions, will change the law or offer some kind of incentive to encourage developers to build and sell on a Commonhold basis. Then we have to convince the most risk-averse and caution institutions. High Street lenders.

Leaseholders' statutory rights

- Under Commonhold and Leasehold Reform Act 2002, leaseholders have the following statutory right to buy the freehold of their property and extend the lease by up to 90 years.

Buying the freehold

- The lease must be for residential purposes; with at least 2 flats. Also, no sub-letting is allowed if you want to buy the freehold.
- At least 2/3rds of the leases in the block have to be for at least 21 years.
- No more than 25% of the building's floor space must be devoted to commercial use (for example, shops on the ground floor).
- At least 50% of the block must agree.
- If the property has been converted to flats, then there has to be more than 5 units to qualify.

Extending the Lease

- Available to those who hold a long lease.
- Extend by up to 90 years.

"I FORGOT. POKER THIS AFTERNOON."

Covenants

- These are conditions of title imposed by an earlier owners or builders.

Positive covenant

- States what an owner/occupier must do.
- E.g. maintain a certain boundary. Usually, the fences/boundaries that you must maintain are shown in the title deeds.

Restrictive covenant

- States what an owner/occupier must not do.
- E.g. conduct a business from the premises.

Neighbours may force nursery to shut using 1938 rule

Lucy Osborne

ONE of Britain's top-rated nurseries could be forced to close, leaving more than 30 families without childcare.

Piplings is one of many businesses in Forest Hill covered by a 1938 covenant that states no trade can operate from a domestic property except doctors, dentists and lawyers.

The antiquated rule affects properties on the Tewksbury Lodge Estate where a number of neighbours are taking legal action against the family-run nursery.

Citing "noise" and "inconvenience", they say it is in breach of the covenant and must close.

If their case succeeds it is feared it would set a precedent affecting up to 100 other home-run firms, such as music teachers, child-minders and consultants.

Piplings was set up by Emma Lee, 36, and husband Philip, 50, in Liphook Crescent in 2010, with planning permission from Lewisham council. Last June Ofsted rated it outstanding and placed it in the top one per cent of nurseries.

Mrs Lee, who has three children aged under four, said: "It is outrageous that a nursery which provides a good service to the community can be victimised by a few neighbours with nothing but a chip on their shoulder." In May or June Central London County Court is set to hear the neighbours' application for the covenant to be enforced. The couple say they have already paid almost £70,000 in legal fees.

Nursery supporters are trying to persuade the neighbours, who are backed by the local residents' association, to stop legal action, and have set up a petition at friendsofpiplings.wordpress.com.

Parent Jason Syrett, 41, said: "We'd all be devastated to lose Piplings. It's like a home from home."

A Lewisham council spokesman said that when planning permission was granted "councillors considered a nursery would have little impact on the environment and be beneficial to the community".

"A restricted covenant... was relatively common in the Thirties. This covenant only applies to the Tewkesbury Lodge Estate. It is a matter for estate residents not the council."

Owners: Emma Lee (in striped top) and husband Phillip with parents at Piplings nursery

Easements

- The right of the owner of one piece of land (the dominant tenement) over the land of another (the servient tenement), e.g.:
    - Right of way.
    - Right to light or prospect.
    - Right to ventilation.
    - Right to hang a sign on another house.
- Onerous easements will be detailed in the Charges register at the Land Registry.

Cheap for a Reason — Public footpath

The coincidentally newsworthy name of Beckham Cottage has already deterred one potential buyer from viewing this country property at Branscombe in East Devon, according to the selling agent, Richard Addington, of FPDSavills (01392 253344). "I suggested the name could easily be changed if desired."

Less easily altered is the public footpath that runs along the drive, passing just 15 yards in front of the house. Getting a footpath officially diverted is difficult. A shame, since the four-bedroom house has an idyllic position in a secluded valley near a pebbly beach, set in 4.1 acres and sheltered at the rear by its own woodland. It faces west: great for G&Ts on the terrace at sunset while taking in the lovely country views.

Although Addington has never seen anyone strolling along the public footpath which leads up the valley, he reckons its existence knocks about 10 per cent off the property's price (it has already been reduced from £600,000 to £575,000).

It may also have been slow to sell because the original cottage has been rebuilt and extended, lending it a modern feel, yet it needs updating. Compensations include a large drawing-room plus a second reception room, a studio space in the garden, private water from a spring, private drainage, and maturing woodland of Douglas fir. Enough to ensure continual interest in the property, says Addington.

Beckham Cottage, Devon A public footpath appears to stand between it and a sale

"But something is putting people off," he adds. "Not everyone wants walkers passing by." A sentiment with which Posh and Becks might sympathise.

CHRISTINE WEBB

Land Registration

- Land registration is the process by which the State guarantees the validity of a title in a registry.
- When land is registered, it makes conveyancing easier, because a search of the register confirms the quality and nature of the title beyond doubt.
  - Originated in 1897.
  - The main legislation is the Land Registration Act 1925.
  - The Land Registration Act 2002 and 2003 has made further changes.
- Since registration takes place when land is legally transferred, unregistered land will not become registered land until its next change of ownership.
- It's estimated that 25% of land remains unregistered.

"MOTHER STILL LEAVES A LIGHT ON FOR ME."

Property register

- Title number.
- Written details.
- Plan of the property.

Proprietorship register

- Ownership and the nature of the title:
  - Absolute – clear title established.
  - Qualified – some conditions attach to the title.
  - Possessory – if the deeds are lost – can be converted to absolute title after a period of 12 years.
  - Good leasehold – Title to the freehold is unknown although everything else is in order.

Charges register

- Details of charges over the property, e.g.:
  - First Mortgagees.
  - Rights of second mortgagees.
  - Spouses' interests under the Family Law Act.
  - Official receiver charges.
- Charges can be registered at the Land Charges Register even if the property is not officially registered.

Unregistered Land

- More difficult for a conveyancer to establish good title and costly to register as a search must be made over the previous 15 years. This is because:
    - A person who has continuously occupied land can claim that land as of right if it can be shown that the owner knew of his presence and did nothing to remove him.
    - The "squatter" can register possessory rights after 10 years, but Land Registry rules provide that a further 2 years must elapse before the title becomes absolute.
- Rights over unregistered land can be registered through the Land Charges Registry. The most common ones are:
    - Second mortgages, not protected by deposit of title deeds, i.e. puisne mortgages.
    - Class F – notification of spouse's interest under the Family Law Act 1996.

Adverse Possession

- Changes have been made in the Land Registration Act 2002 and 2003. Once adverse possession has been applied for, the "squatter" must hold this title for a further 12 years before they can apply for absolute title.

Squatter's rights turn farm widow into millionairess

Judge admits reluctance as he awards family ownership of prime land they used for grazing, reports Peter Foster

A FARMER'S widow stands to become a multi-millionaire after the High Court granted her squatter's rights over 57 acres of prime development land in the Berkshire commuter belt.

Caroline Graham was granted possession of the land, which lies between the towns of Thatcham and Newbury, because her late husband, Michael, had farmed the land, next to his own, for more than 12 years.

If planning permission for housing were granted, local land agents estimate its current value at between £750,000 to £1 million an acre compared with just £2,500 on the agricultural market.

However, even as he made his ruling, Mr Justice Neuberger conceded that his decision, though correct in law, was both "illogical and disproportionate" and did not accord with the principles of natural justice.

He immediately granted the owners leave to appeal.

Three years ago Mrs Graham and her husband, who was killed in a shooting accident in 1998, staked their claim to four fields that they had used since 1984 for grazing cattle at their farm at Henwick Manor, Berks.

The land was among 230 acres purchased for £250,000 in the mid-Seventies by J A Pye (Oxford) Land Ltd, a firm of residential developers who had originally earmarked it for development.

Shortly afterwards, the firm sold 165 acres to a local farmer but retained the disputed 57 acres because of its "development potential".

The land is classified as "White Belt" according to Berkshire county council but is situated in a prime site for any future expansion between Newbury and Thatcham, where a boom in the local job market has created huge pressure on housing.

From 1977 to 1983, Pye granted "grazing licences" to a succession of owners of Henwick Manor Farm, allowing the four fields to be used for grazing, hay and silage.

In 1982, John Graham, a well-known local farmer, had bought the farm at auction for his son, Michael, who married Caroline in 1987.

The judge said John Graham always knew that the disputed land was no longer part of the farm when he bought it and made approaches to J A Pye.

However in 1984, the company refused a grazing licence to the Graham family because it wanted to keep the land "in hand" as it was anticipating seeking planning permission to develop it.

Despite the refusal of the licence, the Grahams continued to use the land as before, grazing their herd of between 80 and 140 cattle each year between February and November and harrowing, rolling and manuring the land to maintain the pasture.

In evidence, the Grahams said that they had "never vacated the disputed land" because they were not asked to do so and "just kept farming all year round".

The Grahams continued to use the land as before until December 1996, when a survey team asked permission to inspect the land, which was on the route of a proposed Thatcham Relief Road.

In June 1997, concerned that the relief road survey "might cause damage to their interests", the Grahams registered "cautions" at the Land Registry, claiming ownership of the land on the grounds that they had farmed it for more than the 12 years required under the 1980 Limitation Act.

That claim by Caroline Graham and her father, Charles Denton, was grudg-

ingly upheld in the High Court by Mr Justice Neuberger. However he made his feelings of discomfort at the decision very clear.

"As may be apparent from one or two passages in this judgment, this is a conclusion which I arrive at with no enthusiasm. It seems to me that it is a result which does not accord with justice and cannot be justified by practical considerations."

Mr Justice Neuberger then explained his reasoning, adding: "If, as in the present case, the owner of land has no immediate use for it and is content to let another person trespass on the land for the time being, it is hard to see what principle of justice entitles the trespasser to acquire the land for nothing from the owner, simply because he has been permitted to remain their for 12 years.

"To say that, in such circumstances, the owner who has sat on his rights should therefore be deprived of his land appears to be illogical and disproportionate."

Solicitors for J A Pye said

Blunders let squatters keep £½m council home

REPORTS BY
BY DAVID MILLWARD

A GRADE II listed house in London is to be handed over to three squatters who have lived in it for more than 30 years.

Their claim to take over the freehold of 49 Calthorpe Street, Clerkenwell, will not be contested by Labour-controlled Camden council.

The "Calthorpe Street Three" – Agoshaman Ceribel, 71, Umiak Mahoupe, 50, and a friend known as Anne – will become the legal owners of the five-bedroom house. It is worth, according to Camden's valuers, between £425,000 and £475,000, despite being in "fair to poor condition".

They claim the property was left in poor repair by the previous council tenants who moved out some time before January 1973. While other squatters from the 1970s moved on to more conventional living arrangements, the Calthorpe Three stayed put, even though their renovation attempts did not impress the town hall.

In November 1983, the council gained a court order granting it possession of the building. Bailiffs went to the house to execute the warrant, but for some unexplained reason did not do so.

Camden made a second attempt to regain the property in 1990, but was turned down by the courts.

After that the authority's housing department ignored advice from lawyers who said it should begin gathering information which could justify another eviction attempt.

In 1993 the housing department was given further legal advice to start new proceedings. Despite two reminders from counsel, nothing was done.

Since then Camden appears to have written off any claim to the house and last year the squatters issued a writ asserting that they should be registered as the legal owners.

"We are holding up our hands to this one," the council spokesman said. "But things have moved on a great deal over the last couple of years. We are now an efficient, well-run authority." He said the council was carrying out an audit of the rest of its property, but he was confident that squatters were not living in any other municipally-owned home.

However the council's gen-

Anne, one of the Calthorpe Three, squats on the doorstep at No 49

Mortgage Law, Policy, Practice & Markets

The Grade II listed house where council inefficiency has allowed squatters to claim the freehold

erosity has not been welcomed by neighbours, who are still expected to pay rent or a mortgage on their dwellings.

"I think it's disgusting," one nearby resident said yesterday. "I think the council is right out of order. It is all wrong. I don't get my home free, I don't see why they should. I wish someone would give me a half-million pound home."

Piers Wauchope, the leader of the council's Conservative opposition, said that the sa was symptomatic of the m aise in the housi department.

"We find it profound depressing that such inef ciency has been allowed to on for so long," he said.

Agricultural Holdings

- Land in rural areas may be affected by the conditions of the Agricultural Holding Act 1948.

- Special care needs to be taken if the security for a mortgage loan has agricultural restrictions.

- Extra security is given to tenants of agricultural land, which might cause problems for the lender in the event of forced repossession.

- Additionally, penalties can be enforced if the land is not properly managed, and this gives rise to the restriction that the land can only be sold to people within the agricultural or fisheries trade.

- This can dramatically reduce the market for the house and thus, the resale value, which concerns the lender.

"WHY CAN'T YOU TALK TO YOUR PLANTS LIKE OTHER PEOPLE?!"

Guaranteeing Title

- A contract for sale states whether the vendor is selling with:
    - Full title guarantee;
    - Limited title guarantee;
    - No guarantee.
- Whether or not the property is transferred with full title guarantee, the vendor covenants that he has the right to sell and he will co-operate fully in giving all assistance and information needed to establish and transfer the title.
- Lenders may insist, as a condition of mortgage, that property is transferred with full title guarantee.

Matrimonial Law

Equitable interests

- In addition to legal rights over land, it is possible for equitable rights to arise, i.e. those that are based on the concept of something being "fair and just".

- This is a similar to concept to matrimonial interests but is much broader in that it is not restricted to married couples or to family situations.

- Equitable interests cannot be registered in the same way as matrimonial interests, but may be decided by a court or more simply by agreement between the parties.

- Equitable interests can cause problems for lenders, who may not be aware of their existence. An equitable interest could, for instance, prevent a lender from repossessing a property on which an apparently sole owner had defaulted.

Matrimonial interests

- The law is set out in the Family Law Act 1996.

- There are many cases where only one spouse (often the husband) is the registered owner of what is clearly the matrimonial home, either because such an arrangement was traditional, or because the couple married after the owner had purchased the property.

- "Non-owning" spouses (who may well have contributed to the costs of buying the house) can register their interest with the Land Registry.

- This effectively prevents the property from being sold until the interest is removed.

- Lenders can prevent a charge being placed by getting the non-owning spouse to sign a "Consent to Mortgage."

Chancel Repair Liability

I am purchasing a property in a nearby village and am worried about chancel repair liability. I have been told by a friend that the rules are changing. Is this correct?
— Paul, Bristol

Chancel repair liability has its origins in historical law and means, in some cases, that home-owners are required to pay for the upkeep of parts of their local church.

It is a common misconception that chancel repair liability is coming to an end. The Land Registration Act of 2002 put the onus on parishes to register any legal obligation on properties within their boundaries. The cut-off date for this was October 13.

So, the buyer will be free of liability if the property was sold after this date, and the chancel repair liability had not been registered.

However, the church can still register claims against existing properties in the parish until they are next sold.

And if somebody receives such a property after the October 13 deadline, as a gift, or at a knock-down price, the church may still be able to register chancel repair liability.

I am in the middle of a property chain which stretches to at least five home-owners. My concern is that there is a high potential that the chain could collapse. Is there anything I can do to protect myself?
— Tim, Dudley

Chains are a frustrating part of the house-buying process, and they have significant consequences if they break down. There is little you can do to protect yourself, but a bit of legwork on your part can minimise risks.

Make sure your finance is in place and your searches are completed. Check daily if you can with the estate agent and your conveyancer to be certain nobody is waiting for any answers from you. You might also check, through your estate agent, that other parties in the chain have the necessary paperwork in place. Often one person in the chain is unnecessarily holding everybody else up by forgetting to answer a question.

- "My husband and I are looking to move to a local village. A friend who already lives there has urged us to look into something called chancel repair liability. I have never heard about it. Can you help?" Barbara, Winchester

- The issue of chancel repair liability has been in the press recently, due to a high-profile case in Worcestershire. Homeowners in a village there have faced some issues as a result of this concept.

- Its origins are in historic law. Local religious leaders were given land and had the right to collect payments from tenants deemed to live within their parish. You do not have to live next door to a church for your home to fall within the applicable area, either. The old law states that community members must pay for the upkeep of the part of the church around the altar. A parochial church council, referred to as a PCC, is often responsible for all other parts of the building.

- In the past, this issue has taken people by surprise, particularly when they have not checked whether they are liable during the purchase of the property. But it is something to consider carefully. Past cases have seen homeowners forced to pay hundreds of thousands towards such repairs. The Land Registry will be making it mandatory for chancel repair liability to be registered on all affected properties. But this process will not be completed until next year.

- Discuss your concerns with a conveyancing solicitor. They might be able to shed some light on whether your new house could be affected by this change. There are searches that can be carried out to show an area's potential liability. Also, indemnity insurance can be put in place for your future protection.

- It can be difficult to determine whether a property has chancel repair liability because it may not be noted on property deeds or be the subject of a standard search. Changes to the process from 13 October 2013 provided some clarity

- Parochial church councils must register a notice of chancel repair liability on the Charges Register at the Land Registry in order for a registered property to be subject to a potential liability.

Stamp Duty Land Tax (SDLT)

Stamp Duty on Property

- Stamp duty land tax (or Land and Buildings Transaction Tax in Scotland) is a lump-sum tax that anyone buying a property or land costing more than a set amount has to pay.

- The rate you'll pay the tax at varies based on the price of the property and the type (we'll focus on residential buildings, rather than commercial).

- Sweeping changes to stamp duty were announced in December 2014. Stamp duty has been reformed - the slab system (where you'd pay a single rate on the entire property price) has been swept away, and in its place is a more progressive system.

- From 1st April 2016, the rates for SDLT will be higher if you buy an additional residential property for £40,000 or more in England, Wales and Northern Ireland. Currently, an additional 3%.

- You'll also pay the higher rate if you buy a residential property in England, Wales or Northern Ireland and you already own one outside the UK

Stamp Duty Rates

Stamp Duty Land Tax

The following rates will be charged on the element of the residential property purchase price within each tax band:

Rate	Value of property
0%	0 - £125,000*
2%	£125,001 - £250,000*
5%	£250,001 - £925,000*
10%	£925,001 - £1,500,000
12%	£1,500,001 and over

*First time buyers will be exempt from SDLT on properties with a purchase price of £300,000 or less. SDLT at the rate of 5% will apply to the excess over £300,001 to £500,000. Standard rates apply to £500,001 and above.

Land and Buildings Transaction Tax (Scotland)

The following rates will be charged on the element of the residential property purchase price within each tax band:

Rate	Value of property
0%	0 - £145,000
2%	£145,001 - £250,000*
5%	£250,001 - £325,000*
10%	£325,001 - £750,000
12%	£750,001 and over

*First time buyers will be exempt from SDLT on properties with a purchase price of £175,000 or less.

Land and Transaction Tax (Wales)

The following rates will be charged on the element of the residential property purchase price within each tax band:

Rate	Value of property
0%	0 - £180,000*
3.5%	£180,001 - £250,000
5%	£250,001 - £400,000
7.5%	£400,001 to £750,000
10%	£750,001 to £1,500,000
12%	£1,500,001 and over.

*Not just for first time buyers but also other home buyers in Wales.

Other Stamp Duties

- The rate of stamp duty on shares is ½% unless stamp duty is below £5
- The rate of stamp duty on bearer instruments is 1.5%

Conveyancing

The Buyer's Guide

- Your solicitor will contact the seller (or their solicitors) and ask for the "information pack", which contains 4 key items:
    - Property information form: a standard questionnaire, which will give details of boundaries (and disputes) and other key property information.
    - Fixtures, fittings and contents form: this tells you what is and is not included in the sale of the house. There is often debate about what has been included in the sale (furniture, curtains, etc.), so you should be careful to agree with the seller what you are getting and let your solicitor know if there are likely to be any areas of concern.
    - Title deeds: these documents show that the person selling the property owns it, and secondly set out any rights or obligations that affect the property.
    - Contract: this is drawn up by the seller's solicitor, and sets out the main terms of the proposed agreement, including names and the price.
- The solicitor will then carry out a number of searches.
    - Land Registry to establish title of registered land.
    - Land Charges Registry search to establish charges over unregistered land.
    - Local land charges search to identify road charges, town planning schemes.
    - Commons registration to check that land being sold is not common land.
    - Environmental search to check on contamination.
    - Mining Search to assess the location of any mines, but only in known areas.
- You will then need to negotiate and agree the contract, based on this and any other surveys you have had carried out.
- You next need to get a copy of a mortgage offer (if you are buying with a mortgage) on this specific property (not just an agreement in principle) which will be given once contract terms have been agreed.
- You are now ready to agree a completion date (the date when the house becomes yours) and can exchange contracts along with a deposit. This is no longer refundable if you pull out of the sale. The minute you exchange contracts, the sale is set in stone - you must buy (at the price stated), and the seller must sell.

- Your solicitor now draws up a purchase deed and sends it to the seller's solicitor, and reports to your lender, with the Certificate (Report) on Title and makes a formal request for mortgage funds.

- Your solicitor hands over to the seller's solicitor the remainder of the purchase money (buying price less the deposit you have provided) and in return you receive the transfer document, which is needed to show the house is now transferred to you (and will need to be sent to the Land Registry) and the title deeds, which is the evidence of ownership and sets out the obligations on the owners.

The Seller's Guide

- *Prepare your property for sale*: You and your solicitor prepare the seller's pack.

- *Contract negotiation*: You will now need to wait for the buyer to get ready. They or their solicitor will read the documents and carry out other required searches. They may also get independent surveys done. Your solicitor should be able to answer some queries, but you may be involved in discussing some elements of the fixtures and fittings form.

- *Contract Exchange*: If all of these queries and responses go ok, then you and your buyer will need to agree a completion date (when you will give over the title deeds and move out) and then exchange contracts.

- *Completion*: Your solicitor will now transfer the Title Deed and transfer document to the buyer's solicitor in exchange for the money for the house. This will then be used to repay your mortgage and the fees associated with the sale of the house.

- You then get the remainder, unless you are buying another property.

Estate agents

- Estate agents act as the agent of the vendor, not the purchaser.
- They are usually paid (by the vendor) on a commission basis.
- Typically 1½% to 3% of the sale price.
- There are different payment schemes, and vendors should be clear, which applies:
  - The fee may be paid only if a sale is achieved.
  - The fee or a proportion of the fee may be payable irrespective of whether a sale is achieved.
  - A separate charge may be made for advertising costs, irrespective of whether a sale is achieved.
  - The fee may be a fixed amount rather than a percentage of the sale price.
- Many estate agents charge less if they are given the sole agency, which allows them only to market the property.
- Estate agents' activities on behalf of vendors may include:
  - Taking details of, and advertising, the property.
  - Advising and guiding the client, for instance, on an appropriate asking price.
  - Negotiating with prospective purchasers.
  - Liaising with the client's solicitor.
- In high price and low supply areas, such as inner cities, individuals can act as an estate agent for the purchaser, seeking out the right home for them.
- Online Estate Agents operate solely online and have a lower charging structure and use web portals such as Rightmove to promote their properties.

Auctions

- What are the advantages of buying at auction?
  - Properties are usually offered at Auction at a competitive reserve price.
  - If you are the successful bidder, you know that the vendor cannot withdraw and that the property is yours on completion.
- Should I inspect the property?
  - It may be possible to inspect a property prior to auction. Anyone who is unsure or has doubts about a property is recommended to seek professional advice.
- Do I need a Building Society Survey?
  - A valuation carried out by a building society is only required should you need a mortgage. This and any other financial advice or arrangements must be organised before the auction day.
- What do I have to pay on the day?
  - It is important that you have all finances ready for the day of the auction. Should you be the successful bidder, a 10% deposit will be required on the day.
- Should I insure the property?
  - You will be responsible for insuring the property from exchange of contracts - it is wise to make arrangements in advance.
- What's a Modern Auction?
  - The new Modern Method of Auction creates a transparent market place for the motivated residential buyers and sellers combining the best aspects of traditional auction and private treaty sales.
  - As a result of this the Modern Method of Auction opens the auction market, once reserved for the professional investor or cash-rich buyer up to normal residential buyers, creating a larger market place, more interest and activity than traditional auction.

	Modern	Traditional
Can anyone buy through auction?	Yes	No
Can a property be bought with a mortgage?	Yes	Increased Risk
How long can it take to complete?	56 Days	28 Days
What market is this type of Auction aimed at?	Everyone	Investment
How much will the property sell for?	Market Value	Under Value
Does this method limit Buyers?	No	Yes

House Purchase Process

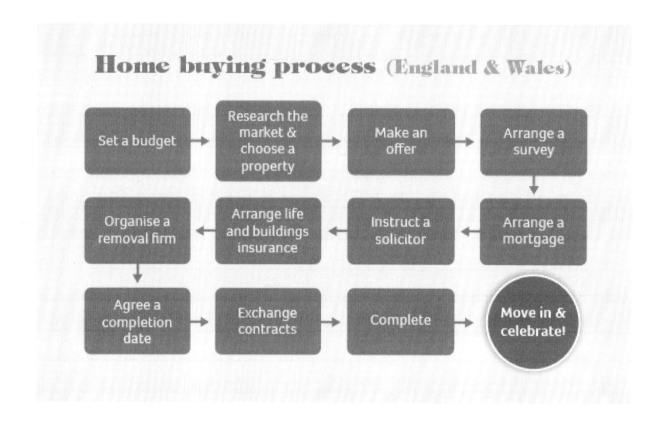

Common Property Defects

Wood-boring insect attack

- Pretty serious stuff this which can destroy wood in the property over time. The picture shows some steps totally destroyed by woodworm.
- The property will need to be inspected by a professional firm specialising in this area and then sprayed with chemicals to kill the woodworm and their eggs. Damaged wood will need to be treated or replaced if seriously damaged.

Damaged rainwater goods

- If left unchecked, the water will run down the walls and possibly penetrate these into the house unless a good cavity has been installed. Older properties built before about 1875 would not have cavities so the water will penetrate inside causing dampness.
- The rainwater goods need repairing.

Structural cracks

- If this were in the house, I would be seriously worried suspecting subsidence or heave. A structural engineers report would be asked for by the surveyor to look into the problem.
- However, it looks as though it is in the brickwork of an outside wall or flower bed.
- If it doesn't affect the main property, I doubt if the surveyor will pick it up.

Defective plumbing

- Unsightly and it would be the water escaping that would damage the property. You can see water on the floor; this will cause damp and decay.
- This would be an undertaking or a retention to get the work fixed.

Parapet/verge wall damage on roof and defective lead flashings

- These are designed to prevent water seeping into the property. If it does it causes damage over time. This will need to be fixed.

Wet Rot

- This is the effect of water coming into the property and damaging wood. This wet rot would have to be stripped out and replaced and the cause of the water seepage fixed ASAP.

Dry Rot

- Dry rot is the result of fungus growth in wood. The fungus soaks up any dampness making the decay look bone dry. But it is devastating and if left untreated can cover the entire property very quickly. Not only damaging to the fabric of property but also to the owner's health.

- Specialist report and action to get rid.

External cracks – subsidence and heave

- Nasty and easy to spot. Subsidence is generally a downward movement causing the foundations to crack and the structure of the property to fail. Underpinning is needed, which effectively fixes the foundations. A massive job.

- Heave is normally upwards movement causing just as much trouble. Caused by tree roots, earth movements downwards such as mining beneath the property.

Rising damp

- A 1970's sitcom or a nasty problem. Caused by having no damp proof course (DPC) or a defective one. This prevents the upward movement of dampness through the porous bricks and mortar. When a DPC is not there, damp rises upwards and can cover entire walls if left unchecked.
- Specialist report and a DPC put in.

Missing and defective tiles

- Here rainwater will penetrate causing damage. They will need to be replaced.

Heave

- Old mine shafts or collapsed earth can cause complete devastation to property.

Japanese Knotweed

- Termendously destructive and impossible to remove
- If it's close to the property, this will cause structural damage.

Oh dear!

- Enough said.

Property Terminology

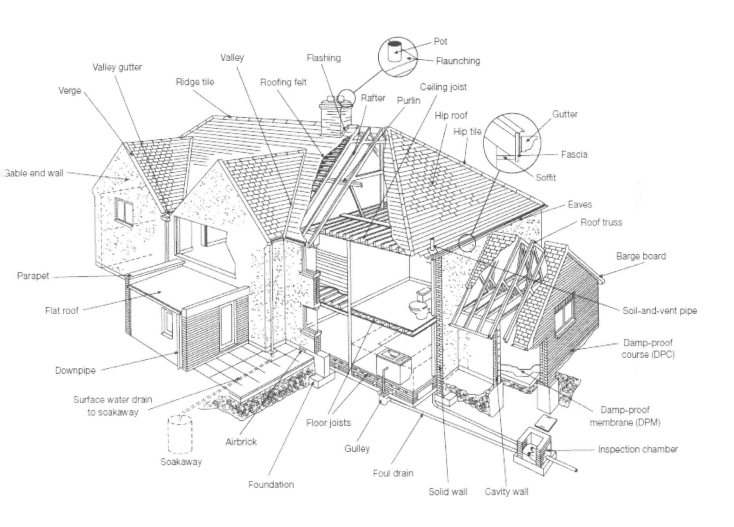

The UK Mortgage Market

Causes of the Credit Crunch

- The economic boom which began in the mid-1990's continued unabated into the 2000's.

- This caused asset values in the Western world to rise dramatically, particularly residential property.

- Lenders in the USA and UK drove to supply finance to enable everyone to live their dream and relaxed their lending criteria to enable more and more people to borrow. Thus the birth of subprime mortgages.

- As house prices continued to increase, the collateral was always good.

- This allowed the lenders to sell off their mortgage books to other institutions who wanted to benefit from the profits without getting involved in lending. Known as securitisation.

- During 2007 the situation worsened. Interest rates began to rise to combat inflation, mortgage payments rose because of this, but also many schemes were sold on a "low start" basis mainly in the USA. Which meant massive increases in payments. This is known as "explosive" mortgages.

- Mortgage defaults rose drastically in the USA, ending the housing boom there. Some mortgage lenders in the USA went bust; many pulled out of lending trying to preserve their capital balance sheets.

- As a result, banks stopped lending to each other preferring to keep the capital to bolster their reserves.

- And more and more borrowers began defaulting, causing the mortgage books to go sour.

- The situation from the USA soon followed for the UK who repeated the chain of events.

- Banks in the UK began to falter and topple and were rescued by the UK government to the tune of billions of pounds.

- All across the world, governments rescued their banking systems.

- Little credit was offered to all borrowers let alone mortgage borrowers, and this contributed to the recession which officially began at the end of 2008.

- Meanwhile, the UK housing market tumbled, in many areas prices fell as much as 25% from their peak in 2007.

The Current Mortgage Market

- This week I've been viewing properties in Cheltenham both for rental and for purchase and chatting to some knowledgeable estate agents.
- Always keen to elicit their views on house prices and the market, I was reminded of some time-honoured principles from the housing market that have been around for decades:
  - Firstly, house prices rise in fashionable areas, particularly property "hotspots"
  - People buy into areas where they can purchase a lifestyle not a house.
  - Local shops help to beef up demand – butchers, restaurants, bars, greengrocers.
  - Rents are designed to increase each year by inflation even if you take out a longer lease.
  - Its not interest rates on mortgages that stoke demand for housing or Brexit.
  - The housing market drives numerous other industries in our country – builders, furniture makers, Homesense.
  - Mortgages are in ready supply thanks to securitisation.
- The fundamental rule for price movement in the residential and buy to let market is…wait for it…supply and demand.
- Presently in Cheltenham, supply is limited. Admittedly it's only January so many properties haven't even entered the market – mine is going on in February – but demand is strong and this is maintaining prices and good homes are going quickly close to asking prices. The buy to let market has a different cycle – tenancies end all year round so the rental market is always at a peak.
- Mortgages, whether residential, buy to let or equity release, will remain in fashion so long as supply is constant and the effect of securitisation and mortgage backed securities fuels this.

Factors affecting mortgage market

- Interest rates.
- Inflation.
- The state of the economy.
- Supply and demand.
- Government policy.

The Mortgage Players

Building Societies

- Although still major mortgage suppliers, building societies have since the mid-1980s diversified into other financial and banking services. They still, however, have to have to confine 75% of their lending to residential mortgages.

- There are now just 44 building societies remaining, the majority either merging to form larger societies or converting to banks.

Banks

- Banks were attracted to the mortgage market by three main factors:

  ➢ Attractive returns. The end of the building societies' cartel pushed mortgage interest rates up to market levels.

  ➢ Low risk. The default rate on mortgages is very low, even in times of economic recession.

  ➢ Cross-selling. A mortgage customer opens up for the bank a long-term opportunity to sell insurance, pensions, investments and other products.

Specialised Mortgage Lenders

- Funded mostly from the wholesale market.

- Often operate on a centralised basis, with few if any branches, relying on intermediaries to sell their mortgages. Many operate wholly on a telesales basis or via the Internet.

- Some tend to operate in niche markets (e.g. people with poorer credit histories).

Packagers

- A good mortgage packager would add value to the process of applying for a mortgage by taking care of the much of the administration and paperwork
- They are not lenders in their own rights, but instead, use a panel of selected lenders.

Sub Prime Lenders

- Focus on the subprime, higher risk borrowers
- They securitise their lending book
- The credit crunch had seen the demise of such lending although recently, they are re-appearing, preferring to call their lending – specialist.

Quit complaining!

Consumer Credit Acts

FCA Regulation of Consumer Credit

- Replaced the OFT – Office of Fair Training – and has wider enforcement powers.
- FCA authorises:
  - Consumer credit lending
  - Credit broking
  - Debt counselling and collection
  - Credit information services
  - Credit reference agencies
- FCA now enforces Consumer Credit Acts
- FCA Conduct rules apply
  - Treating customers fairly applies
  - Authorisation process adapting
  - Approved person regime applies
  - Full investigation, enforcement and redress

Consumer Credit Act 1974

- This Act regulated loan agreements, quotations and advertisements, and other activities of lenders and credit reference agencies.
- It applies to "Consumer Credit Agreements" which are basically loans and other forms of credit with no upper limit.
- Suppliers of credit as defined in the act must be licensed by the Office of Fair Trading.
- Typical Annual Percentage Rate (APR) must be shown. APRs include the interest charge plus all the compulsory charges to give a balanced view of the total charge.
- Clients must be made aware of :
  - The nature of the contract;
  - Their rights and obligations.
- Clients must receive a copy of a loan agreement for their own records.
- Loan agreements must contain cooling off provisions unless they are signed on the lenders premises.
- Credit reference agencies must disclose information held and must correct it if inaccurate.

Consumer Credit Act 2006

- Financial Ombudsman Service incorporates all consumer credit disputes.
- Borrowers can now challenge credit agreements in Court.
- No upper limit for the size of the loan – used to be £25,000.
- Lenders to provide more information throughout the term of the loan.

The EU Consumer Credit Directive

- The Directive has been implemented in the UK under the Consumer Credit Regulations 2010. These provide:
- Changes on the right to withdraw and providing adequate explanations. A 14-day withdrawal is allowed.
- New assumptions for calculating APR.
- Provides new and clearer information to be given to consumers prior to entering an agreement
- New requirements of information to be included in an agreement
- Sets out advertising requirements particularly how the APR is quoted

The Consumer Rights Act 2015

- Supersedes previous legislation.
- Gives enhanced rights to consumers with faulty goods and services.
- Act covers:
  - What to do when goods are faulty
  - How services should be fit for purpose
  - Faulty provision of goods and services
  - Unfair terms in contracts
  - How organisations can respond to breaches of law
  - The act aims to reduce time involved in dealing with consumer disputes
  - Third party arbitrator can be asked to make decision about disputes, in a similar manner to FOS.

Consumer Insurance Act 2012

- The Consumer Insurance (Disclosure and Representations) Act 2012 came into force on 6th April 2013. It removes the duty on consumers to disclose any facts that a prudent underwriter would consider material and replaces this with a duty to take reasonable care not to make a misrepresentation.

- The Act does not currently apply to commercial insurance but will nevertheless have a significant impact on insurance distribution. The Insurance Act of 2015 takes care of the commercial insurance side.

- The Act will abolish the consumer's duty to volunteer facts that an underwriter might consider material - instead, consumers must take reasonable care to answer questions that are asked by insurers.

- The onus now sits squarely with the insurer to ask you the questions that they want to know information about. Instead of a duty to volunteer material facts, now the law requires you to answer the questions that are put to you fully and accurately. You need to "take reasonable care", and one of the factors that will be taken into account is whether the questions asked by the insurer were clear and specific.

- So, forms may get a little longer because the onus is on the insurer to ask you the right questions. Insurers should no longer be making reference to a "duty of disclosure."

Agency Law

- An agent is a person who acts on behalf of someone else (who is called the principal).

- A tied agent or company representative acts as the agent of the product provider, whereas an independent financial adviser (IFA) is acting as the agent of the client.

- In law, the actions of the agent are treated as the actions of (and are therefore binding on) the principal.

- It is therefore essential that the extent of the authority, given to the agent to act on the principal's behalf, should be made clear.

- Apparent authority occurs if an agent acts outside that stated authority, but it can be shown that the principal has given the impression that he has authorised what the agent has done, then it will be binding on the principal.

- Ratification allows the principal to agree the action of the agent after the event.

I KNEW THE BUNGEE CORD OFF THE DECK WOULD CLOSE THE DEAL FOR YOU.

Contract Law

- There are a number of requirements for valid contract. These include:
    - There must be offer and acceptance and consideration
- In house purchase, the consideration is the deposit
- The contract must have a legal purpose:
- The terms of the contract must be certain, complete, and free from doubt.
- For instance, if the subject matter of the contract did not exist, the contract would be void.
- If one party fails to keep to the terms of the contract, the other party has a number of possible remedies:
    - He could simply choose not to perform his part of the contract, although this is often not possible (e.g. the payment has already been made)
    - He could seek damages, i.e. financial compensation for his loss
    - He could obtain an injunction, which is a court order compelling the other party to do something - or refrain from doing it
- Under most contracts the principle of "caveat emptor" - let the buyer beware - applies. This means that there is no duty of disclosure between parties to the contract.
- However, there are exceptions - including life assurance contracts, to which a different principle applies. This is the principle of *utmost good faith*, which means that all material facts must be disclosed.
- A life assurance applicant must, therefore, disclose all those facts which a prudent underwriter might need to know in order to decide the terms on which a policy could be issued.

Energy Performance Certificates

- The Government introduced the Home Information Pack from August 2007 but suspended them from 21 May 2010, ut the legacy is the Energy Performance Certificate

- An Energy Performance Certificate is required when a building is built, marketed for sale or rented.

- The certificate includes a report, which contains:
  - Information on the property's energy uses and CO2 emissions;
  - Recommendations on how to reduce energy use and CO2 emissions.

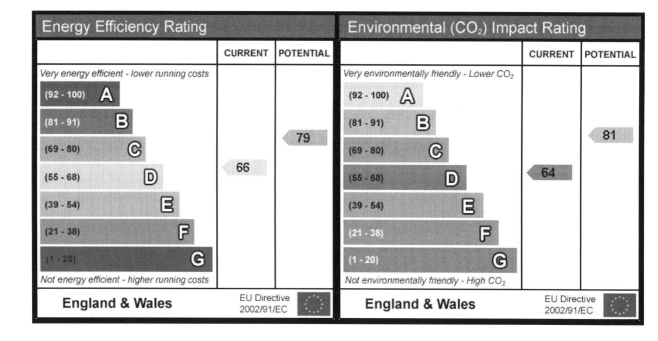

The Consumer Protection (Amendment) Regulations 2014

- Replaced previous legislation intended to control marketing and selling practices and covers all situations where professionals, including estate agents, engage with consumers.

- Gives consumers certain rights and remedies where a firm is in breach of the regulations, and right to redress if they have been subject to misleading or aggressive practices.

- The legislation does not apply to financial services or consumer credit as these are covered by other regulations.

- There are three main parts to the regulations:
    - There is a general ban on unfair commercial practices.
    - Misleading and aggressive practices are minimised
    - There is a 'blacklist' of practices that are banned because they are deemed to be unfair.

- It is a breach of the regulations to fail to disclose information that the average consumer would need to make an informed decision.

- Estate agents are expected to point out important or unusual matters to consumers. For example, significantly exaggerating the dimensions of a property would be providing misleading information.

- If a business fails to follow a code of practice to which it has subscribed, it could be in breach of the regulations.

2 Application for a Mortgage

Assessing the Income

- Many lenders, prior to Mortgage Market Review (MMR), based the maximum loan they offered on multiples of income.

- This could be, for example, 2½ x main income plus 1x secondary income or 3 x sole income.

- Other factors are relevant, for instance, which income is likely to be the most stable in the short-term and/or long term?

- With the MMR and change in MCOB rules from April 2014, more focus is being paid on affordability.

- Lenders need to assess expenditure as essential, standard of living and discretionary.

- Lenders are now wholly responsible for assessing affordability of mortgages.

- Flexibility is needed in the application of income multiples as a young almost-qualified professional with a promising future might get more, whilst a senior person in a faltering industry would not be such a good risk.

- Definitions of employees' income might include basic pay, overtime, commission, bonuses, maintenance and trust income.

- For the self-employed, what matters is ability to service the loan from continuing business profitability.

- The net profits of the business over a period are therefore more significant than personal drawings, which could be distorted by use of an overdraft or other working capital.

Proving the Income

- Salary
  - P60 and payslips for at least three months
  - SA302 from HMRC to confirm income
- Reference from bank:
  - Bank statements can give an overall picture of an applicant's lifestyle.
  - But other transactions could be being hidden in other accounts.
  - If accepted, should cover a suitably long period.
- Lender's reference:
  - Very reliable, but many lenders charge a sizeable fee for providing one.
  - Usually a statement will surfice.
- Landlord's reference:
  - Could be useful to establish ability to make regular payments (rent). Bank statement swill also show this
- Other evidence:
  - Self-employed people may supply:
    - Accounts
    - Tax assessments
    - Business plan

Credit Assessment

Searches

- Electoral roll - to establish whether applicant is living at address given on application form. May not be up-to-date.
- Credit reference searches - should reveal bad debts, insolvency and County Court Judgements.

Credit scoring

- Scores are apportioned to various features of the application.
- Sophisticated and computer-based.
- Based on historical data relating to risk.
- E.g. if employed people have been a lower risk than self-employed, they will be given a higher score in relation to that feature.
- Scoring can easily be changed if changes in experience warrant it.
  - Advantage – decisions can be made at a relatively low staff level.
  - Disadvantage – may remove the human element and the use of discretion.

"IT'S THE FIRST OF THE MONTH. YOU EMPTY THE GARBAGE AND I'LL EMPTY THE CHECKBOOK."

Advised Sales Rule Changes

- From April 2014, the overriding principle is that borrowers should always receive qualified advice
- This removes the option for a firm to offer a non-advised sale.

Execution-only

- Individuals can opt for execution only, provided they have done so at their own request, and they understand the consequences of losing the protection of the advice process
  - High Net Worth and professional customers - minimum annual net income of £300,000, or minimum net assets of £3 million.
  - Mortgage Professionals
- Where the service is through 'non-interactive' channels, such as internet or postal sales
- Those customers who are looking to vary the terms of an existing mortgage, either with their current lender or by moving to a new lender may be dealt with on an execution only basis as long as the loan amount will not increase. •
- Rejected advice - if a customer has rejected the advice given and wishes to take out a different mortgage on an execution-only basis, the firm can arrange that as long as the MCOB rules on execution-only sales are satisfied.

Interest only mortgages

- Firm must make sure customer demonstrates they have arranged a clearly understood and 'credible' repayment strategy that the lender has assessed at the time to have the potential to repay the capital at the end of the term.
- Acceptable repayment methods could include investments with a defined benefit, downsizing or the allocation of regular bonus payments to pay down the capital.
- Speculative strategies such as relying on house price inflation, potential inheritance, windfalls or ad-hoc investments are not credible.
- A new version of interest only mortgages has been agreed by the regulator involving loans to those in retirement. These do not need the strict repayment vehicle requirement since it's the sale of the house that will repay the loan.

Mortgage Disclosure

- Customers must be in a position to make an informed decision and have time to think it through.

- Selling any product or service ought to adhere to this – mortgage advice makes it mandatory and requires that firms disclose information at various points in the sales process.

Initial Disclosure

- Given out on the first client meeting and outlines the services offered.

- No longer a requirement to issue a written IDD for non-distance mortgage contracts such as face to face sales, you have to give the "key messages" verbally and document on the file that disclosure has been given.

- You'll hear about MCD mortgages and non-MCD mortgages – this is just a technicality as disclosure relates mostly to new mortgages which are all MCD (taken out after 2016). The only exception is where an existing mortgage is varied with a further advance; this would be non-MCD.

ESIS – or European Standard Information Sheet

- Is required for all new mortgages, but lenders may adapt their existing KFI and call it the plus version. Plenty of information is needed to comply, and it must be issued soon after the mortgage advice is given; definitely, before the application is made.

  - ESIS period and lender details
  - The broker involved
  - The loan – amount, currency, term, rate, property value
  - The interest rate in the form of the APRC – Annual Percentage rate of Charge
  - Payment frequency
  - Monthly payment and warning around affordability plus interest only repayment vehicles
  - Other obligations from the borrower
  - Early repayment rights
  - Length of the reflection period
  - Complaints

Application for a Mortgage

County Court Judgments

- When a person cannot pay his creditors, a civil case can be brought against him in the County Court.

- The Court can make a judgment against the debtor, which remains in force until the debt is repaid.

- It is a criminal offence to conceal such judgments from a lender.

"WE'RE PHASING OUT YOUR POSITION, PARKER."

Fraud and Fraud Act 2006

- Fraud is deliberately attempting to obtain funds by dishonest means.

- Mortgage-related fraud includes:
  - Identity theft fraud
  - Occupancy fraud – where the applicant declares owner occupation but will rent the property instead
  - Income fraud
  - Employment fraud – claiming a non-existent job
  - Failure to disclose liabilities or debts
  - Valuation fraud – a home's value is purposely overstated,
  - Shotgunning - This is where multiple loans for the same home are obtained simultaneously for an amount in excess of the actual value of the property.

- Measures to combat fraud include:
  - Dealing only with reputable intermediaries and with solicitors, accountants, and valuers with a known track record.
  - Detailed follow-up of information about income and outgoings (written and telephone).
  - Particular attention if applicant is self-employed (SA302's or accounts signed off by reputable accountants?).
  - Use credit bureau checks, and searches of other registries and databases.
  - Install proper audit systems.

The Fraud Act 2006

- The Fraud Act 2006 includes the offences of false representation and failing to disclose information where there may be a legal duty to disclose the information, as in a mortgage application.

- The value of a mortgage gained in this way will be regarded as proceeds of crime under the Proceeds of Crime Act 2002, and the borrower will be regarded as having committed a money-laundering offence.

Money Laundering

- The Financial Conduct Authority is now responsible for Money Laundering and this has significant influence for mortgage lenders and brokers since people will attempt to launder ill-gotten gains through house purchase and sale.

- The Money Laundering Reporting Officer (MLRO), must be occupied by someone of appropriate seniority

- All staff must be made aware of and given regular training about, what is expected of them under the money laundering rules, including the consequences for the firm, and for themselves, if they fail to comply

- All firms must take reasonable steps to ensure that their procedures are up to date and reflect any findings contained in periodic reports on money laundering matters issued by the government, or by the Financial Action Task Force

"Why couldn't we embezzle the money like everyone else?!"

Buying and Selling Costs

Selling Costs

- Solicitor's conveyance fee for arranging the sale of your property. Drawing up the contract and exchanging.
- Estate Agent's fee. For sole agency expect to pay typically 1% to 3%. For multiple agencies, you pay 4% or more.
- Mortgage redemption penalty if you've been caught within the redemption period. All mortgages have a sealing fee.
- Energy Performance Certificates
- Removal Fees

Buying Costs

- Solicitor's conveyance fee for arranging the purchase of the property
- Stamp Duty
- Disbursements
    - Investigation of Title i.e. Land Registry search and commons search
    - Local Land Charges Search
    - Commons search
    - Mining Search
    - Environmental searches
- Survey Costs

Mortgage Costs

- Solicitor's legal fees for the lender. Liaising with the lender, drawing up the Certificate of Title and completing the Mortgage Deed
- Mortgage valuation fee
- Arrangement fee £50 to £2000
- Reservation fee £100 to £1000
- Broker's arrangement fee
- Bankruptcy search
- Telegraphic transfer fees

Search Changes at the Local Level

- Local Authority Searches or Local Land Charges, call them what you like, they're essential to any purchaser. Until now, they've been taking an inordinate amount of time and have held up many a house purchase.

- Why are they officially called local land charges? Simply because they are restrictions or obligations on a piece of land such as planning permissions, listed buildings. Conservation areas and tree preservation orders.

- Each local authority maintains a register of charges, and many are still in paper format. Searches can take up to 30 days and come in just shy of £100.

- The cavalry have arrived. MH Land Registry launched last month its digital Local Land Charges Register (LLC) with one local authority and expects up to 26 other local authorities to follow suit.

- Unfortunately, Cheltenham local authority hasn't been earmarked, so I'm going to spend an afternoon at their offices shortly to carry out my own search for the conveyancing of a terrace house I'm currently buying.

- It'll take time for all the local authorities – there are 326 of them – to migrate their data, but it won't be long until this time-wasting search is done instantly online.

CON29M – Mining Searches

- Its staggering how many homes are affected. 29% of all homes are in coalfield areas, and that doesn't include the other minerals that have been dug out of the ground in the last 1,000 years – salt, tin, chalk, brine…the list goes on.

- Britain's Industrial Revolution was underpinned by coal mining as this fuel drove our economy for hundreds of years. We're only just ridding ourselves of King Coal preferring cleaner energy solutions.

- There are two types of mines at play here. For the past hundred years, we've had deep mining where considerable volumes of coal are extracted deep underground. These mines have been well documented by the Coal Association and monitored too.

- The main issue here for property owners is subsidence. If you remove a large chunk of the earth deep underground, it will cause movement above. This creates subsidence and claims approaching £10 million have been paid out in the last two years.

- The second type of mining is altogether different, dangerous and costly to homeowners. That's the impact of shallow mining which has occurred unregulated and unrecorded for hundreds of years prior to the deep extraction processes. Some of these mines are a mere metre or so below you. Almost 3 million homes are situated above these identified mines. How many are above anonymous mines, is not known.

- The problem for owners here is one word. Sinkholes. You've seen these in the news. Photos of large holes in the ground where the topsoil or road tarmac has just fallen in creating a cavernous hole in the ground. Rarely do actual properties fall into sinkholes, although that does happen, the biggest issue for homeowners is access. Each year more than 500 sinkholes appear across the UK blocking roads and access to properties. A huge sinkhole in St Albans in 2015 denied access to four owners for over two years.

- These mine entry points can be vertical shafts which haven't been capped correctly or documented at all and can proliferate in areas know for mining.

- The lesson for mortgage advisers is to know your area and be able to briefly explain the need for a search. Conveyancers will deal with this, naturally and the Law Society has just opened this up to outside firms who have speeded up the process considerably.

- And you may wonder where your next door neighbour's cat has gone.

Assessing the Property

Basic valuation

- Carried out on behalf of the lender but borrower pays the fee.
- Purpose is to assess adequacy of property as security for mortgage.
- Fairly superficial inspection carried out.
- Report to lender:
  - Value for lending purposes;
  - Whether suitable as security;
  - Insurance value;
  - Any repairs needed.
- When making an offer based on the basic valuation, the lender will disclaim any responsibility for the condition of the property and the suitability of the purchase price.

Condition Report

- Brought in to help buyers on a budget receive a decent report on the condition of the property.
- It differs from the lender's valuation in a few ways:
  - It is designed for the borrower, not the lender
  - It doesn't attempt to value the property or give an insurance figure
  - It contains some recourse in the event of negligence on the surveyors part
- The report is limited but more in-depth than the valuation.
- It uses a traffic light system to advise how serious the condition is – red for serious and so on
- A typical cost for a home worth £250,000, the Condition Report would come in at £200, but you will also need a valuation for the lender

Buildings Survey

- Thorough and complete inspection of the property.
- Maybe commissioned by borrower for own peace of mind. Either way - paid for by borrower.
- Carried out by professional surveyor or architect.
- Expensive but generally worthwhile.
- If property proves defective, borrower could sue surveyor for negligence.

Home buyer's report

- Halfway stage between basic valuation and full structural survey.
- Limited in scope, but should show up more serious defects, which might lead a potential buyer to turn down the property or make an amended offer.
- Very limited comeback in the event of negligence.

The Survey Results

- The survey will confirm details of the property:
    - When built;
    - Dimensions;
    - Tenure;
    - Valuation for mortgage purposes;
    - Valuation for insurance purposes;
    - Evidence of subsidence or heave;
    - Narrative report on the property;
    - Disclaimer regarding limited nature of survey carried out.
- Acceptance – the property is good value for security for the loan being asked for.
- Conditional acceptance, subject to:
    - Undertaking - by the borrower to carry out certain repairs or alterations within a certain time.
    - Retention: of part of the advance until the borrower has carried out certain repairs to the lender's satisfaction.
- Lower advance - the Valuer considers the property of lower value than the price.
- Further investigation - more detailed survey required before decision can be made.
- Decline - not suitable security for mortgage purposes.

"MY MOTHER WILL STILL BE ABLE TO FIND OUR HOUSE ..."

Factors Affecting Property Value

- Tenure
  - The vendor must have undisputed title.
  - Freehold flats may not be considered because of problems with common areas such as stairs.
  - Leasehold property must have a specified minimum unexpired period on the lease, beyond the end of the mortgage.
- Condition
  - Obviously, the condition of a property affects its value.
  - If possible, the condition should be compared with that of any similar properties in the locality whose value can also be known.
- Location
  - For example, properties in, or even near to, some inner city areas known for violence and crime, may have lower values.
- Environmental factors
  - Examples which may affect value are:
    - Radon: a naturally occurring radioactive gas;
    - Proximity to a nuclear power station;
    - Overhead power lines.
- Method of construction
  - The materials used to build a property clearly affect its expected life and its value.
- Design
- Quality of construction
  - For new properties, builders should if possible be members of the National House Building Council (NHBC), whose Buildmark scheme protects against all defects for two years and major defects for the next 8 years.
  - NHBC has a limit of £1,000,000 for new build.
  - Zurich's cover extends to 15 years but was withdrawn in 2009.

Property Value

What puts value on a house, and what makes it lose value? We have six properties now to illustrate this.

High Rise Flat

- Location – North London, ex-local authority flat, in mix of high rise and low rise property both local authority and private.
- Fourth floor
- Lift
- Construction – re-enforced concrete construction. Built 1960's
- 2 bedroom
- Leasehold – 123 years remaining
- Price £125,000
- No vacant possession

- The main concern on value and mortgage purposes would be its ex-local authority nature. This is not snobbish (I grew up in a council house) but re-saleability for the lender. Fourth floor is better than 14th floor, and there is a lift. Many lenders would not have this kind of dwelling on their lending books.

- Construction wise well it's not standard and concrete block work has deteriorated over the years leading to demolition. Many thousands of these properties were built by local authorities in the 50's and 60's.

- Lease is fine; however you would want to check the lease conditions.

- No vacant possession means that there is a tenant in the property so this would be a buy to let property not suitable for personal occupation.

- The price certainly reflect these factors.

- As far as the surveyor is concerned, I doubt if it were to get to the stage of valuation since the lender would probably refuse it before it went to application.

Flat above a shop

- 2 bedroom leasehold flat above commercial premises on the High Street
- Tube 1 mile away
- Location North London
- Traditional construction and built 1890's
- 78-year lease remaining
- No allocated parking
- Separate rear access
- Needs internal re-decoration
- Full vacant possession

- More mainstream property and lending situation this one. Flats above shops are not uncommon, particularly in cities such as London. They are sought after and offer good value for money. This one has all the right ingredients a lender would look for. Own access is essential and only minor decoration, which would be asked for by the surveyor with an undertaking.

- The lease is quite short, but as long as there is at least 30 to 40 years remaining after the mortgage term had expired, this should not be a problem.

- Insurance would be a challenge because by being above commercial premises, this creates more of a fire risk, but because it is leasehold, the freeholder will have a "block" insurance policy covering all the flats in the parade.

- Parking is not a deal breaker, just a big headache if you have a car, but being close to the tube may be an advantage someone is wishing to take in lieu of parking.

Application for a Mortgage

Thatched Listed Property

- Semi-detached Grade 2 Listed property with 4 beds over 3 floors
- Freehold with vacant possession
- Needs finishing internally
- Public footpath through the back garden
- Thatched roof
- Sale by auction with guide price of £250,000

- A beautiful looking property but looks can be deceptive. Nothing that would prevent a mortgage being secured present. The thatch roof does have a more limited lifespan than slate and tile, but they do make property desirable.
- It's a huge property for the price so I would think the price reflects the semi nature and the fact that it is Grade 2 Listed and needs finishing works.
- This grading would put many buyers off because improvements and alterations are strictly monitored by English Heritage, which aims to ensure materials and such are like for like. Grade 2 dominates the majority of listed properties in the UK and describes the property as of special interest.
- It just might put some people off so the lender would want to make sure the new owner gets these works finished to make the property readily re-saleable. A substantial retention would be imposed possibly a complete retention until the works are completed.
- The easement, i.e. the footpath, is a fact which is reflected in the price. It happens in the countryside, and little can be done about it. This can put some people off and will affect re-saleability.

Timber Property

- Timber constructed property on an island on the River Thames
- Restrictive covenant preventing permanent occupation and only to be used for leisure and weekend retreat purposes.
- River frontage.
- Leased by the Environmental Department

- Quirky property and definitely not suitable at all for mortgage purposes.
- The construction is totally unacceptable. It isn't timber frame but made of sheets of timber. It's a glorified garden shed.
- Flooding is a major and definite risk, so buildings insurance would be impossible to obtain.
- Access to the property looks tricky except by boat, which is probably its market.

Application for a Mortgage

Ex Local Authority

- 3 bedroom mid terrace house – ex-local authority.
- Newly built conservatory/extension in the rear.
- Traditionally constructed, i.e. bricks and tiles
- Freehold
- Shared access through the tunnel beneath the property
- Built 1950's

- This property is ex-local authority with a conservatory built on after purchase from the council.
- The surveyor will advise that the planning consents and building regulations approval documentation for the conservatory is checked by the solicitor before completion.
- The general condition looks fine, but the surveyor will advise on this.
- The only concern could be the tunnel entrance to the rear seen on the photograph. This tunnel is for the owners of the two mid-terrace houses to gain access to their rear gardens and is a common feature on these types of property.
- The tunnel allows for shared access, but they are normally an example of flying freehold. This is where some of your actual property hangs over someone else's land. Typically above the tunnel is one of the owners' properties, and this hangs over the land which belongs to someone else.
- Typically, not a major problem if the total floor space that's flying is less than 25%.

New Build House

- New build yet to be completed
- Restrictive covenants not allowing high fences in the front or the parking of commercial vehicles or caravans in the front.
- Main road behind property separated by earth mound
- Freehold of traditional construction.

- Some issues here. Firstly the surveyor will ask that the property be subject to an NHBC guarantee. This gives protection to the owner (and the lender) for ten years of faults developing on the property. For the first 2 years, pretty much any problem is fixed. These are called snags in the trade and Barratts (the builders) will have a special team who will go around fixing these "snags" for free.
- The remaining 8 years is an insurance-based cover which looks at major faults only.
- The whole mortgage loan will be retained until the property is completed and the surveyor will want to re-inspect the property when this is done.
- The customer can exchange contracts, but the mortgage completion will be delayed until the property is finished.
- All the usual consents and approvals will need to be seen as well.
- New build estates often have these covenants which ensure the frontages are clean, minimal and attractive to future purchasers. Often builders will take people around just finished estates to give them a feel for their new property, which hasn't yet been completed.

Application for a Mortgage

"Rent a Roof" Solar Panels

- Solar Panels on roof
- Property roof leased to external company for up to 25 years
- Feed in Tariff (FIT) in operation
- Onerous Easements on roof

- Consumers who have installed solar panels under a 'rent-a-roof' scheme may struggle to sell their homes and risk breaching their mortgage arrangements, the Royal Institute of Chartered Surveyors (RICS) has warned.

- Free solar schemes, also known as rent-a-roof schemes, provide free electricity-generating solar panels to householders. The householder benefits from the free electricity, while the company installing the panel keeps the cash usually earned by the householder from the government's feed-in tariff, which pays people for generating their own energy.

- Rent-a-roof leases often run for up to 25 years without a break clause, and RICS says that homeowners could be discouraging potential buyers and creating structural problems for their property by having them installed.

- A minority of lenders will not lend on properties with "Rent a Roof."

Planning consent

- The story of the farmer who built a Mock Tudor castle without planning consents and then surrounded the home with straw bales to escape unnoticed was famous. Unfortunately, Google Maps allowed Surrey County Council to spot it and have it torn down.

- Planning Permission or Consent is a general requirement that all alterations to properties plus new build must have the permission of the local authority planning team.

- There are permitted rights, which allow owners to make certain improvements and alterations without permission, but these are not allowed in designated conservation areas, areas of outstanding natural beauty, national parks or heritage sites. Our home in Cheltenham is in a conservation area, and when you look at the roofs, not one house has a roof extension, and there are over 500 houses in our area. They're simply not allowed.

- Permitted rights, though, give the homeowner the ability to improve and alter without permission, but they still may need building regulations approval. These rights were improved back in 2013 to boost the building sector while the UK languished in recession, but these are only temporary.

Permitted Rights

Garden Shed

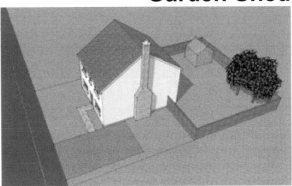

- Planning permission NOT required as.
    - Located to rear of property.
    - Does not exceed 4 metres in height.
    - Does not exceed 2.5m in height when closer than 1m to boundary.

Loft Conversion

- Planning permission NOT required as roof windows only.

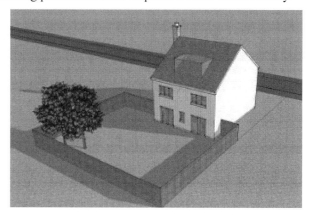

- Planning permission NOT required as dormer is rear facing. Dormer does not exceed half the width of existing roof. Not within 10m of boundary facing roof.

- Planning permission required as dormer to front elevation. Within 10m of boundary. The above examples are for guidance only; other conditions may apply.

Conservatory to Rear

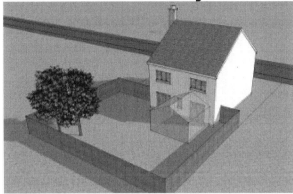

- Planning permission NOT required as located at rear of property. Not larger than 24m sq or 20% of original ground floor area.

Conservatory to Side

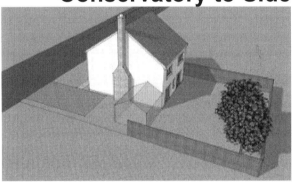

- Planning permission NOT required as not forward of the front elevation (elevation facing road). Not larger than 24m sq or 20% of original ground floor area.

Conservatory to Front

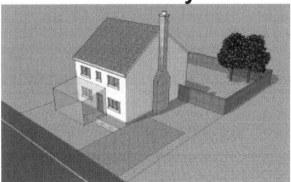

- Planning permission required as located at front of property.

Extension to Rear

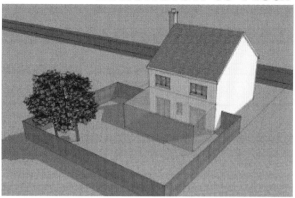

- Planning permission NOT required as located to rear of property. Not more than 4 metres in depth. Not more than 4 metres in height (overall). Not more than 3 metres to eaves.

Extension to Front

- Planning permission required as located to front of property.

Side Extension

- Planning permission required as located within 10m of boundary.

Fences and Walls

- Planning permission NOT required as fence or wall is lower than 1m. Fence or wall not more than 2m and back from front elevation.

Garage Conversion

- Planning permission NOT required. Not part of a listed building. Not in a conservation area.

Garage

- Planning permission NOT required as located to rear of property. Does not exceed 4m in height. Any part of garage within 1m of boundary does not exceed 2.5m.

Porch

- Planning permission NOT required as under 3m sq. Not within 2m of boundary or road. Not more than 3m in height.

- Planning permission required as within 2m of boundary or road.

Planning Consent Procedure

- Planning consent proof is a vital ingredient to anyone who buys a property that has already been extended. Both the new owner and the lender will insist upon consent documentation otherwise the council could tear it down later. Not good if you hold a substantial mortgage on it.

- Applying is quite simple, and you can do it yourself:
    - Draw up plans of your building work, many employ an architect
    - Submit to the council with the fee
    - The council will advertise what you are doing online and on lamp posts
    - They will grant full planning or outline planning, which is subject to the detail being confirmed later on.

Building Regulations

- These are overseen by the local authority but deal with a completely different matter – construction quality, health and safety and energy conservation. They are needed in addition to the planning consents and involve a detailed break down on how the work is going to proceed, designs and materials used.

- Building control then approve it and will investigate the build during the phases and approve at the end that the work was done to specification requirements.

Our Cellar

- Our house is a 1840's period terraced home in a Conservation Area; we can't build up or out, so we plan to build under. The home has a Victorian cellar for coal. Coal is not our heating source anymore, so we're turning it into a habitable room.

- We first engaged a team of architects to draw up some plans on the design including a basement window at the front. We applied for planning for this window and received it 8 weeks' later plus change of use from a coal bunker to a room.

- Having to dig two feet deeper requires underpinning and the drawings of a structural engineer. This person is qualified in building structures, weights, loads and such and advised how this was to be underpinned.

- The waterproofing or tanking expert was then called in to confirm the cellar could be made waterproof.

- These specifications were sent to building control for building regulations approval along with the detailed plan of the cellar. The Building Inspector then arranged a series of visits to check up on the contractors doing to the building work.

- All the work was supervised by the architect and everyone adhered to the plans.

- Success ensued, but 20% of the cost was fees for the various professionals. Seems like an industry ripe for disruption; there seems plenty of profit going round for these professionals.

Listed Buildings

- Having your property designated a listed building may sound glamorous on the estate agent's details but will cause incredible barriers when you want to make changes to the fabric of the property.

- Listed buildings are graded 1 to 3, the vast majority being grade 3. Grades 1 and 2 are generally older and have the most onerous restrictions.

- Listed building consent is required to make alterations.

- Generally, Grade 2 listing allows internal changes but only like for like on the outside whereas grade 1 only allow like for like alterations throughout the property.

Higher Lending Charges

- Traditionally also known as Mortgage Indemnity Guarantee Policies (HLCs).

- Single premium general insurance policies bought by the lender to protect their losses in the event of repossession.

- They are paid for by the borrower but provide no cover for the borrower.

- Used for high percentage lending.

- They can be calculated by establishing a basic advance in which all lending above that figure has an indemnity applied on a straight or increasing scale.

- For example, a lender might stipulate 80% basic advance. They might have two tiers of premium rate. 5% on lending up to 85% and 10% above that.

- Alternatively, some lenders only start charging for HLCs over 90% but calculate the cost based on lending above 75%. Lender may allow the premium to be added to the loan.

- Under ABI guidelines, insurers normally:
  - Insist on certain specified mortgage underwriting standards;
  - Impose 20% excess on claims made.

Subrogation

- The HLC policy insures against the possibility of loss for the lender.

- It does not remove the borrower's contractual obligation to repay the whole debt.

- If a lender claims on a HLC policy, the insurer has the right to sue the borrower for the amount it has paid. This is called the right of subrogation.

Other Security

Life assurance policies

- Endowment policies acquire a surrender value - although they may have no value for anything up to two years, and the surrender value will normally be less than the premiums paid for much longer than that.
- Lenders may consider such policies as additional security.
- The policy may be assigned to the lender, who becomes the legal owner of the policy.
- Alternatively, the lender may just take a deposit of the policy. This gives no legal right but may create an equitable right.

Collateral deposits

- A sum of money placed with the lender as additional security.
- The funds are effectively frozen until the debt is repaid or reduced to a point at which the additional security is no longer necessary.

Other security

- Lenders can take other forms of security, including guarantees by other people, although building societies are limited in the nature of acceptable security by the Building Societies Act 1986 as amended by the Building Societies Act 1997.

Offer of Advance

- Often the sigh of relief document for difficult lending decisions.
- This is the formal written statement by a lender that it is prepared to make an advance to a borrower.
- It forms the basis of the terms and conditions of the contract that will be made between lender and borrower.
- It is not itself a contract, and it is not binding on the lender. Many people feel lenders cannot withdraw the offer after it's issued, but they can.
- In practice it would only be withdrawn if:
  - It was discovered that false or misleading information had been given in the application;
  - The borrower's circumstances had changed;
  - The value of the security had changed.
- In addition to basic details of the borrower, an offer of advance will contain:
  - Details of property;
  - Address and brief description;
  - Details of tenure;
  - Value for mortgage purposes and for insurance purposes;
  - Details of loan offered:
  - Amount;
  - Term;
  - Interest rate and whether fixed or variable;
  - APR;
  - Repayment method;
  - Repayment amount;
  - Mortgage indemnity guarantee details;
  - Any other terms and conditions (e.g. clawback).
- Binding offer
  - The lender's final mortgage offer must be binding.
  - This does not prevent a lender from making an offer that is conditional on the borrower meeting certain (lawful) requirements or the lender gathering further information.

Standard conditions

- Lender's right to withdraw offer.
- Lender's right to vary offer.
- Property must offer vacant possession.
- Lender does not give any warranty as to condition of property or appropriateness of purchase price.
- Subject to satisfactory title.
- Acceptance before specified expiry date of offer.

Specific conditions

- Conditions that are unique to particular cases:
  - Completion of roads and access;
  - Payments in stages (for self-build cases);
  - Subject to final inspection;
  - Undertaking by borrower to complete specified repairs in specified period;
  - Retention of some proportion of loan pending essential works;
  - Subject to "consent to mortgage" form signed by all occupants over 17 who are not party to the mortgage.

"THAT'S THE ONLY HOUSING START I'VE SEEN ALL MONTH!"

Mortgage Deeds

- Known also as the legal charge – it is the main way of creating a mortgage in England and Wales.
- Could be referred to generically as mortgage deeds.
- The mortgage deed is a binding contract between lender and borrower.
- It is normally linked to a set of mortgage conditions, often referred to in the deed but set out in a separate document or booklet.
- The deed and related conditions will contain the following:
  - General details
    - Details of lender and borrower;
    - Description of the property;
    - The charging of the property to the lender as security for the loan;
    - Details of all monies due: capital, interest, charges, fees etc.
  - Borrower's covenants
    - To make payments as required by the contract;
    - To keep the property in good repair;
    - Not to sublet without the lender's consent;
    - To comply with the law and with local authority requirements;
    - To comply with the property covenants;
    - To comply with lease conditions, if leasehold;
    - To insure the property to the lender's satisfaction.

The Mortgage Deed Lender's Rights

- To call in the mortgage.
- To make charges as specified in the deed and conditions.
- To insure the property if the borrower fails to do so.
- To meet conditions imposed by statute, local authority or title, if the borrower fails to do so, and to make appropriate charges.
- To consolidate.
  - ➢ If a borrower has two mortgages with the lender, secured on two different properties, the lender can treat them as one loan covered by the total security of the two properties.
- To let the property as mortgagee in possession.
- To transfer the mortgage, subject to the borrower's consent.
- To apply the legal remedies, i.e. repossession proceedings.

Property Insurance

- Lenders invariably insist that the borrower takes out property insurance.
- Both parties are concerned that the value of the property should not be affected accidental damage, natural disasters and other perils.

Lender's rights

- A property is insured, and the insurance continuously maintained.
- Its interest as mortgagees is noted on the policy.
- They have a right over any claim, to ensure that the money is used to remedy the subject of the claim.

Reinstatement Cost

- The valuer provides this to reflect the re-building costs of the property.
- This bears no relation to the value.
- It broadly represents the amount of money required to temporarily re-house the owners whilst the property is demolished, the site cleared, foundations repaired and the property re-built with the original specifications.

Typical cover

- Standard cover on a property insurance typically includes the following:
    - Fire, explosion, lightning, earthquake;
    - Storm and flood;
    - Subsidence; heave and landslip
    - Escape of water, or frost damage;
    - Leakage of oil;
    - Damage by falling trees;
    - Riot and civil commotion;
    - Malicious damage;
    - Impact by aircraft, vehicles, animals.

Block Policies

- Administered by the lender.
- Insurer establishes criteria for acceptance of cover. Maybe branded with lender's name.
- Lender cannot insist that borrower takes this cover unless the mortgage is a special offer. May include contents cover at a specified proportion of buildings cover.
- Premiums usually collected by Direct Debit, possibly together with the mortgage payment.

Advantages to the borrower

- Quality of cover usually high.
- Adequate cover at all times.
- Simplicity of cover and payment arrangements.
- Premiums may be cheaper due to simplified administration.

Disadvantages to the borrower

- Standard approach may not meet some specific needs;
- Higher value properties (and contents) may not qualify;
- Commercial properties not usually covered.

Advantages to the lender

- Increased commission.
- Branded product.
- Economies of scale.

Panel of insurers

- Many lenders have a "panel" of up to eight or nine insurers, with whom they have long-standing agency agreements so that they can offer a choice to borrowers.
- The Office of Fair Trading's guideline is a minimum of three.

Artificial Intelligence and Mortgage Advising

Credit Scoring

- Credit scoring is teeming with AI. Your client's ability to obtain a mainstream mortgage is entirely determined by their credit score and the big three – Experian, Equifax and TransUnion – use advanced AI to embrace the client's history and to predict whether they will pay their mortgage or not. Humans don't make this decision – AI does.

- Your AML provider – Anti Money Laundering – will use machine learning and cloud trawling to activate a score which decided whether someone is a risk of money laundering. They search the internet using AI to find out whether your post is being redirected – a significant determinant of AML – whether you've exchanged some significant amounts of Euros recently, or have sold a house without reinvesting the proceeds.

- All AI and a bad score can scupper your mainstream mortgage application. As a mortgage broker, this is pleasant music to your ears as you can re-broke the case to a specialist lender who can listen with human ears.

- Mainstream lenders – High Street Banks and Buiding Societies – are moving into AI-based applications. Since the financial crash, they have industrialised their mortgage processing and de-risked it as much as possible. No humans are needed. Thank you. Mortgage Brokers have a bright future.

Product Selection Tools

- Product selection tools have been around since 1988; my first one merely displayed lots of logos to the customer – we called it the MSS Mortgage Selection System – it was a fabulous selling tool on my 1980's IBM computer screen. However, its ability to source the loan was diddly squat – completely useless.

- Nowadays, we have the usual culprits of Mortgage Brain that can select the right mortgage using traditional selection criteria, but real AI is entering the space. Twenty7Tec and others are revolutionising the rules search engine. Key in your customer is self-employed for two years, has a partner on a zero-hours contract and has state benefits plus maintenance from their ex-husband, and the new AI will spring into action.

Connecting with Clients

- Not AI, but impressive technology. We use Skype, Facetime, Zoom; not tethered to the phone anymore. Ubiquitous social media has to appear here. AI is present when you recommend contacts on LinkedIn. Live streaming using Facebook or YouTube. Many advisers are talking to large groups of people with these technological marvels.

- On the horizon is virtual reality and augmented reality, and these really will be game changers and not so futuristic as people think. Apple is rumoured to be bringing out a very stylish device for their iPhones. Let's be brutal – the majority of VR headsets look very geeky – the Apple design will be fashionable and desirable. They'll do what they did to mainstream the SmartPhone.

- VR devices will revolutionise video calling, making it as though you are in the client's front room.

CPD and Self Development

- Advisers are receiving a helping hand in their quest for self-development, and this sector is getting very Artificially Intelligent. The PFS, the arm of the Chartered Insurance Institute (CII) have introduced personalised study streams with AI curating a tailored study plan for you according to your experience, qualifications, age.

- The CII is curating an enormous collection of online video and resources to help members achieve their CPD, and the search capability utilises AI. It will suggest videos to members as they log on. It'll monitor the background and studying the member has already achieved and begin to recommend a pathway.

- Later Life Academy – AIR Sourcing – Answer in Retirement – are releasing interesting, intelligent learning systems for members.

Suitability Reports

- These most dreaded of reports – on the adviser's side – are finally being spruced and delivered using artificial intelligence. Gone are the templated monsters of the past, in are the tailored, chatty computer generated reports that customers are delighted to read. Bespoke and personalised, they feed off of the factfinder system and data collected by the adviser.

- Future systems will use APIs to connect to social media and the wider web to eliminate the need for a factfind. The adviser will merely run a discussion around the factfind's content to discuss needs and priorities.

Client acquisition

- Already heavily automated. Database marketing, inbound marketing and the use of social media help advisers find and keep new clients. Automated software can rummage the web looking for ideal candidates according to demographics, geography and needs.

- The message for you? Embrace AI, use it, take advantage of it. Don't fear it; successful advisers will incorporate it into their practices to ensure their clients receive the pinnacle of advice.

- "Alexa, what's for my supper?"

3 Mortgage Payment Methods & Products

Capital and interest mortgages

- Also known as repayment mortgages, or occasionally as annuity mortgages.
- They form the great majority of all mortgages.
- Each monthly repayment consists partly of interest and partly of capital repayment. In the early years, this is almost entirely interest, but over the years, the proportion of capital increases.
- Typically it takes about ¾ of the term before the repayments are more than 50% capital.
- The capital outstanding therefore, decreases slowly at first, and more quickly later.
- If the correct repayments are made throughout, the loan will be fully repaid at the end of the term.

Benefits to the borrower

- Easy to understand.
- Amount of capital outstanding decreases, therefore attractive to those who like to see their debt decreasing.
- Easy to top up, subject to status and security.
- Life cover for the decreasing debt is normally cheap.

Limitations to the borrower

- Life cover not built in.

Interest-only mortgages

- The borrower pays interest to the lender throughout the term.

- The capital is repaid in full at the end of the term.

- Making regular contributions to a long-term investment product such as an ISA, endowment policy or a Personal pension normally makes repayment of the capital.

Benefits to the borrower

- Life assurance is built in on endowment policies (but not ISA's and Personal Pensions).

- Additional term life cover for ISA or pension mortgages is usually cheap.

- Lump sums from the investment (repayment) vehicles are usually tax-free.

- There is the possibility of a surplus at the end of the term after the loan has been repaid.

Limitations to the borrower

- With most repayment vehicles, there is no guarantee that the maturity value will reach the figure necessary to repay the loan.

- They are therefore unsuited to customers who are risk-averse.

- Many repayment vehicles, especially life policies, may have no capital value for the first one or two years.

- The schemes can be complex and less easy than repayment mortgages for the borrower to understand.

- Can be relatively inflexible, e.g. difficult to reduce payments if a borrower is in financial difficulties.

- No capital is paid off during the term (except in the sense that the repayment vehicle is building up a capital value).

Retirement Interest Only (RIO)

- For those of you old enough to remember the lyrics or you're a fan of 80's music, will know this comes from Duran Duran's seminal album which went to number two in the album charts in May 1982.

- A new innovation which the FCA have embraced for all mortgage advisers is the interest-only mortgage designed for the elderly marketplace.

  - Applicants are usually age over 50
  - No end date, the outstanding loan is payable by the sale of the property on death or moving into a care home

With Profit Endowments

Non-profit endowment

- Fixed premium for a fixed (guaranteed) sum assured on death or at the end of the term.
- Very few investment policies are now issued on this basis.

With-profit endowment

- For a higher fixed premium, the policyholder gets not just a guaranteed minimum sum assured, but also a chance to share in the company's profits, by means of added bonuses.
- Reversionary bonuses
  - Normally added annually, and, once added, cannot be removed.
  - Maybe simple (based on the sum assured) or compound (based on the sum assured and previously-added bonuses).
- Terminal bonuses
  - Added only at the point of claim, on death or maturity.
  - The rate can be increased or reduced to reflect the success or otherwise of stock market investment by the company.

Low-cost with-profit endowment

- The guaranteed sum assured is set at such a level that the bonuses expected to be added would be sufficient to raise the claim value to a certain level after a specified period.
- This is normally used for mortgage purposes, with the aim being that the final claim value should be equal to the mortgage amount.
- Additional life cover is added so that the death claim value is always at least equal to the projected final value.

Unit-linked Endowments

- Unit-linked endowments are suitable for investors who:
  - Prefer a more direct link to stock-market type investments;
  - Are willing to accept more investment risk (without guarantees) for the chance of making greater gains;
  - Wish to have control over the particular type of investments for their policy.
- Premiums paid are (possibly after the deduction of certain expenses) allocated to purchase units in a chosen fund or funds at the appropriate offer price.
- A pool of units builds up, and these units are cashed in at the appropriate bid price to:
  - Pay the ongoing expenses of running the policy as described in the policy details;
  - Pay the costs of providing any life/sickness cover which the policy provides – known as mortality and morbidity charge;
  - Payout the surrender, maturity, or death claim value when the policy ceases.
- The level of charges to cover expenses is much more visible on unit-linked policies than on with-profits policies. They may include some or all of the following:
  - The bid-offer spread on the price of units;
  - A regular monthly policy fee;
  - An initial nil-allocation period during which premiums are not allocated to purchase units;
  - An initial period in which the units purchased are "capital units", which suffer higher annual charges than the normal units (and therefore are slower to increase in value).

Unitised with-profit endowments

- This product is suitable for clients who like the guarantees provided by with-profits policies, but who would like to explore the possibility of changing the risk profile of the investment element of the policy.

- The concept of unitised with-profits lies somewhere between with profits and unit-linked.

- The pricing structure is similar to that of unit-linked policies, except that management charges are not explicit.

- As with traditional with profit policies, unitised with-profits contracts are entitled to bonuses which depend on the performance of the company's life fund:
    - Bonuses are added either by increasing the unit price or by allocating additional units to the policy.
    - Once added, bonuses cannot be taken away - i.e. unit prices cannot fall except in the case of surrender (see below).

- Unitised with-profit policies give a guaranteed minimum amount payable on death or maturity.

- This amount is usually based on a minimum annual percentage rate of growth on units of the unitised with-profits fund.

- If the unit value is greater than this, the larger amount is paid.

"Harris here is looking after Childrens' Accounts."

Endowment Shortfalls

- Many endowments sold in the late 1980's and early 1990's had relatively high predicted growth rates.
- At the time, these were very achievable.
- High growth rates meant lower premiums, and in a competitive market, the lowest cost often got the business.
- These predictions, with hindsight, have been wildly optimistic and many of these policies are projected to produce returns well below the mortgages they secured.
- Where a shortfall is predicted, the customer can:
    - Switch part or whole of their mortgage to a capital and interest basis;
    - Repay the shortfall with a lump sum or increased monthly contributions;
    - Take out another repayment vehicle such as a Unit Trust ISA;
    - Extend the term of the endowment if it is unit linked;
    - Increase the endowment premium or set up a new additional one.

Individual Savings Accounts ISAs

- A government-backed savings initiative for the masses, giving tax benefits.
- Maximum annual investment £20,000.
- Additional Permitted Subscription allows surviving spouse or civil partner to make additional ISA subscription to the value of the deceased's ISA holdings
- Individuals can split the annual allowance amongst cash, equities or innovative finance ISAs

Equity ISA

- Includes shares, unit trusts, Gilts, OEICs, Investment Trusts, REITs and Child Tax Funds.
- Minimum age 18.
- No CGT or income tax on dividends
- The maximum investment in 2019/20 is £20,000.
- Individuals can invest in any combination of cash and/or stocks and shares ISA

Cash ISA

- Building Society, Bank Accounts and National Savings.
- Minimum age 16.
- Tax-free interest.

Withdrawals

- Withdrawals at any time and can be replenished during the tax year.

ISAs and Dying

- Death is a certainty; few people know what will happen to their Instagram account on death and even fewer what will happen to their ISA.

- Each year ISAs have the maximum investment adjusted, but recently the main ISA has stuck to £20,000. Many allow you to withdraw and then top up to the same limit. Help to Buy and Lifetime ISAs have strict maximum funding.

- Little is known what happens on death because we all die at some point.

- On death, your ISA can benefit from Additional Permitted Subscriptions which allow the survivor to pump money into your ISA for up to three years. 180 days following the estate being wound up, if you have stocks and shares ISA.

- The money invested is still protected from all income and capital gains tax, so not too a shabby deal.

- However, I'm still not too sure what will happen to my Facebook profile when I die.

Junior ISA

- Available to children under age 18 who didn't qualify for the Child Trust Fund, therefore, no government contribution

- Anyone – family, friends – can contribute up to £4,368 per annum

- Invested in cash or equities in a similar manner to ISA

- Income tax-free but no withdrawals until aged 18

Innovative Finance ISA

- The new Innovative Finance ISA allows individuals to lend money through FCA-regulated and approved peer-to-peer lending websites

- Also known as peer-to-peer lending platforms.

- P2P is 'crowdfunding', a rapidly growing form of lending.

Help to Buy ISA

Mortgage Payment Methods & Products

Lifetime ISA

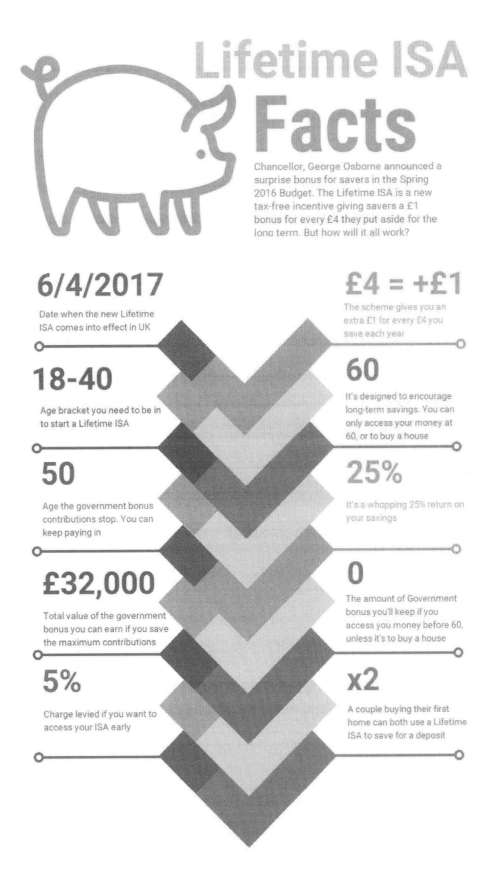

Personal Pension Plans

Personal Pensions

- Where you read personal pensions you should be thinking stakeholder pensions – they are broadly the same.

- They are available to any UK Resident under the age of 75. This is employed people, self-employed, unemployed, children – anyone.

- The most someone can contribute to their stakeholder pension is 100% of their annual income or £40,000 whichever is the higher figure.

- However, you can carry forward unused allowances for up to 3 years.

- There is also a life allowance restricting the fund to £1,055,000.

- The pension fund will accumulate free of income tax and capital gains tax on investment gains.

- Contributions are paid net of basic tax for everyone, whether they pay tax or not. Higher rate taxpayers recover the balance through their self-assessment.

- Other Stakeholder features:
    - An annual charge of no more than 1.5% of the fund for the first ten years, then 1% thereafter.
    - The minimum contribution to a stakeholder pension cannot be more than £20 and contributions can be weekly, monthly or at other intervals, or can be single, one-off, contributions.
    - They have the ability to stop and start contributions without penalty.

- You can take your benefits from age 55. You can take up to 25% of your pension fund as a tax-free lump sum.

- The rest of the fund is used to buy an income (an annuity) which will be taxable. You can use an Open Market Option to buy the best annuity on the market.

Contributions

- Contributions to the Personal Pension are capped at £40,000 or your income whichever comes first. This prevents people putting too much in.

- If you're not earning or can't prove income, the limit is £3,600 each year. You can also bring forward the previous 2 years' unused allowances if you have a large sum to invest.

Fund Growth

- Growth of the fund is also capped. Called the Lifetime Allowance, you can't build up a pension pot of more than £1,055,000 from April 2019. Although this seems like a huge sum, it does have an influence on the money at retirement.

Death

- If you die before age 75 and you haven't taken your pension, the fund is returned to your beneficiaries free of tax.

- Dying after age 75 will incur a tax charge on the remaining pension pot as it transfers to your beneficiaries.

Options at age 55

- Tax-Free Lump Sum
    - Up to 25% of the whole fund, can be taken as a tax-free lump sum. Traditionally, this was the amount that was geared towards repaying an interest-only mortgage.

- Uncrystallised funds pension lump sum
    - This means taking the whole pension pot as a lump sum. How tempting is this, but you'll need to bear in mind that the whole sum (excluding the 25% tax-free part) is liable to your marginal rate of tax. Remember it's the whole sum, so this would very easily push a non-taxpayer into high rate tax.
    - Pension Linked Mortgages can now gear themselves to the entire pot, not just the 25% tax-free element, although the tax charge is quite hefty. I can see a few people repaying their mortgages in this manner.
    - You can take smaller lump sums when you want to, after age 55. These would also be taxable, but with some careful planning, you might minimise this.

- Flexi Access Drawdown (FAD)
    - We live in a world with too many acronyms – I mean, FAD!
    - Here you can take your 25% tax-free lump sum, and then draw off an income from the actual pension pot. The income is taxable but the pension pot remains invested, and you can still contribute if you wish (up to £4,000 per year).

Term Assurance Policies

Level Term Assurance

- Sum assured remains level throughout; therefore, real value may be eroded by inflation.
- There is no maturity value and no surrender value at any time.
- Level annual/monthly premiums or single premium.
- Uses – family protection, key person insurance, cover for loans, debts.

Decreasing Term Assurance (Mortgage Protection Policies)

- Commonly used to cover loans such as mortgages or hire purchase.
- The sum assured decreases over the term in line with the reduction of the capital outstanding on a repayment mortgage at a specified rate of interest (often known as a mortgage protection policy).
- Can be single life policies, or joint life first death.
- Premiums are lower than for level term assurance.
- Premiums are level even though the sum assured reduces.
- Premiums are often payable for the full term but are sometimes restricted to 2/3 or 3/4 of the term.

Convertible Term

- Life cover is the same as normal term assurance.
- Contains option to convert to permanent policy (whole life or endowment) for up to the same sum assured without further medical evidence.
- Premium before conversion around 10% to 15% higher than normal term assurance premium.
- Premium after conversion is the standard rate for the age at conversion.
- Useful for people who:
  - Want to begin a policy taking advantage of current good health;
  - Want a more permanent contract but cannot afford the premiums yet.

Renewable Term

- Typically 5 or 10-year policies.
- They can be renewed at the end of the term without further evidence of health, i.e. a similar policy is issued for the same sum assured, but the premium is now that for the age at renewal.
- Again, useful for those wishing to keep initial premiums to a minimum.

Increasable Term

- The option exists, without evidence of health, to increase the cover on a specified date or dates, or when extending the term under a renewability option as described above.

Personal Pension Term Assurance

- Pension Term Assurance is virtually the same as level term assurance except you can get up to 45% tax relief on the premiums.
- Policies written before December 2006, retain their tax relief. Policies written after this date do not qualify.

Variable Rate Mortgages

- Due to intense competition in the mortgage market, very few new loans are taken out a pure variable rate basis.

- This mortgage is linked to the lender's standard variable rate or SVR (but you knew there would be an acronym here).

- Variable mortgages are usually taken out if a substantial discount or cashback is available.

- Discounts allow a reduction in the lender's normal mortgage rate over a period of time.

- Nothing is owed at the end of the discount period, unlike the deferred interest mortgage of the past.

"AND IF YOU KEEP A MONTHLY MINIMUM BALANCE OF ONE THOUSAND, YOU ALSO ARE CONSIDERED TO BE ONE OF OUR BANK VICE-PRESIDENTS."

Base Rate Tracker Mortgages

- A variant of this mortgage is the Tracker loan. This loan tracks or follows a set interest rate such as the Bank of England base rate.

- This rate is set each month by the Monetary Policy Committee of the Bank of England.

- Tracker mortgages are normally combined with flexible arrangements.

- Another rate that some loans track is the LIBOR – the London Interbank Offered Rate.

Fixed Rate Mortgages

- The rate of interest is fixed for an initial period of the loan.

- This is an advantage only if interest rates rise during the fixed rate period.

- A booking fee or arrangement fee is paid by the borrower (typically £100 to £2,000).

- This is to secure funds at a fixed rate of interest.

- After the fixed rate period, the loan reverts to a variable rate of interest.

- The borrower will have to pay redemption fees in the event of early redemption.

- These may be expressed as a number of months' interest.

- Their purpose is to dissuade borrowers from redeeming the loan if interest rates fall.

- The redemption fee period may be longer than the fixed rate period.

Capped Mortgages

- Similar to fixed-rate mortgages except the rate of interest charged can fall below the capped rate but not go above during the capped term.

- Older style versions also had a collar which was a lower rate which prevented the interest charged falling below this figure.

- Have you ever bounced a really bouncy rubber ball in between the floor and ceiling? Watch how it just goes up and down but never above the ceiling or below the floor. Same concept.

LIBOR-related mortgages

- London Inter-Bank Offered Rate (LIBOR) is the rate at which banks lend to one another.

- It is a key indicator of the short-term price of money.

- Some lenders offer mortgages at interest rates linked to LIBOR.

- The interest rate is reviewed at specified intervals and adjusted in line with changes in LIBOR. Typically reviewed every 3 months.

- Not often used for residential mortgages although, in the current credit crunch climate, some lenders are looking to base their tracker mortgages on LIBOR rates.

- More common for loans secured on commercial properties.

Cashback Incentive

- An incredible inducement and difficult to refuse.

- A Cashback is a sum of money paid by the lender to the borrower on completion of a mortgage based as a percentage of the loan.

- The cash is an incentive to take out a mortgage at a time when personal finances may be tight.

- It is often particularly attractive to first-time buyers.

- Cashback is currently between £200 and £500 much less than in the past when it could have been as much as £10,000

- The factors which tend to lead to the larger cashbacks are:
  - Larger loans;
  - Smaller loan-to-value ratio;
  - Clawback.

- In offering a cashback, the lender is effectively discounting the product against its income-generating potential over the whole term or a large proportion of it.

- It, therefore, needs a way of encouraging the borrower to maintain the loan over a substantial period.

- This is normally achieved by means of clawback:

- If a borrower redeems a cashback loan early (normally within the first five years, though periods vary), some or all of the cashback has to be returned by the borrower.

- It is essential that borrowers are made aware of the possibility of clawback before they take up a mortgage with clawback - they will almost certainly have spent it!

Guarantor Mortgages

- A shift recently has allowed many lenders to offer Guarantee Mortgages.

- These simply add a guarantor to the mortgage deed, which gives the lender someone else to call upon in the event of the borrower's inability to pay the monthly instalments.

- In addition, lenders can offer larger income multiples to enable the first time borrow to take a larger loan.

- Guarantors are normally relatives of the borrowers, you can have more than one, but their age mustn't be more than 65. Affordability checks are made on them.

Right to Buy Mortgages

- Used to help tenants buy their local authority home.

- Since 1980, tenants who have lived in a council house for two or more years or in another 'right to buy' property belonging to certain public bodies, have a right to buy it at a substantial discount.

- The latest legislation is the Housing Act 2004 which brings in new tenants whose tenancy started after 18 January 2005. Those whose tenancy existed before this date are known as existing tenants.

- The Deregulation Act of 2015 amended qualifying periods for England exclusively.

New Tenants

- These tenants gain the Right to Buy after 3 years of a tenancy in England, Wales and Northern Ireland.

- The maximum discount is 35% for houses and 50% for flats in both England and Wales/Northern Ireland.

- Right to Buy ended in Scotland in 2016

- House buyers qualify for a further 1% for every year above the minimum tenancy, to a maximum of 70%.

- Flat buyers qualify for a further 2% to a maximum of 70%.

- If the house is sold within 5 years, a proportion of the discounted price has to be returned. After that, the house can be sold freely.

Right to Acquire

- Similar scheme but designed for housing association tenants to buy their property.

Self-build Mortgages

- Find a piece of land and build a home to suit your dreams. You can with a self-build mortgage.
- Lenders spread out the payment of the loan over the building period. These are known as stage payments and are generally paid in three or four instalments.
- Maximum (loan to value) LTV of 75%.
- Self-build projects carry with them some additional concerns for lenders, in particular:
  - The commitment of the borrower to see the project through;
  - Method of construction and quality of building work;
  - Ability to remain within budget.
- These can be countered by:
  - Appropriately timed release of funds.
  - Regular inspections of progress and quality of work.

Stage Four – utilities, plumbing etc

Stage Three - Roofing

Stage Two Outer Shell

Stage One - Footings

Flexible Mortgages

- With the increasing popularity of the repayment mortgage and the need to satisfy consumer's demand vehicles for the next century ensured we had flexible mortgages.

- Their flexibility results from the following common features:
  - Irregular payments facility – including overpayments, underpayments and payment holidays;
  - Additional borrowing facilities.

- Underpayments and payment holidays are restricted by the amount of overpayments the borrower has previously made. Additional borrowing facilities are agreed in advance up to a mortgage to value limit, often 75% to 80%.

- A key feature of flexible mortgages is their treatment of interest, which is calculated on a daily basis. Borrowers, therefore, benefit immediately when overpayments are made.

- Competitive pressures have resulted in most lenders providing flexible facilities with no early redemption fees or charges.

Off-Set Mortgage

- A variation of the Flexible mortgage is known as the Off-Set Mortgage. The current account and mortgage account balances are offset against each other for the purposes of calculating interest on a mortgage.

- Some also combine a savings account as well.

- This means that the interest you pay on your mortgage is totalled each day to take account of your total debt so any current account or savings account balance will offset your mortgage debt.

Buy To Let Mortgages

- Previously, buying a property to produce an income was considered by lenders to be a commercial undertaking.

- Therefore, mortgages on property intended to be let, have attracted higher interest rates than those available to owner-occupiers.

- Also, rental income was not usually allowed to be considered in the assessment of a borrower's ability to repay the mortgage.

- Things changed in the late 90's and 00's, and many lenders consider the buy to let market lucrative with good loan to value lending and low repossession rates.

- Buy to Let mortgages are available for between 5 and 45 years and for up to 80% of the property value.

- Through a Buy-to-Let mortgage, the rental income you get for the property is used to finance the mortgage.

- Lenders will expect landlords to use a letting agent to manage the property and for the tenants contracts to be drawn up as Assured Shorthold Tenancies.

- Your gross rents should be approximately 145% of your monthly mortgage repayment.

- Single rooms being let in the main residence of the borrower are usually of no concern to the lender. This is known as lodging.

Changes in Buy to Let Lending

- Since 2015, the government has introduced a variety of changes to the Buy to Let market to discourage small landlords and encourage first-time buyers entering the market.

- Before 2017/2018, you could use the interest you pay on your mortgage each year to offset your tax bill. Landlords could claim relief at their personal tax rate, up to 45%

- In a nutshell, landlords will no longer be able to deduct the cost of their mortgage interest from their rental income when they calculate a profit on which to pay tax.

- The Government will allow a tax credit equivalent to basic rate tax (20pc) on the interest

- The tax increase, will be phased in from 2017 and fully implemented by 2020 in a reducing scale

    - 2017 – 2018 – loss of 25% high rate relief
    - 2018 – 2019 – loss of 50% high rate relief
    - 2019 – 2020 – loss of 75 high rate relief

- The 10% wear and tear allowance was removed and replaced by "Furniture Replacement Relief."

- Stamp Duty for second time home purchasers has risen by 3% across all the bands, and the old higher capital gains tax rates still apply to second properties.

- A conversated attack on landlords which has given rise to the Limited Company route becoming popular with landlords as this keeps some of the tax advantages.

FCA Regulation on Buy to Let Mortgages

- Advising on, arranging, lending and administering consumer buy-to-let mortgages is subject to a legislative framework, as set out in the Mortgage Credit Directive Order 2015.

- When determining whether a transaction is a consumer buy-to-let, the key factor is whether the client has ever lived, or plans to live, in the property.

- Inherited properties which are rented out are also deemed consumer Buy to Let and regulated.

- If the buy-to-let loan is genuinely for business purposes and a property has been purchased with the sole intention of letting it out (and the borrower has never lived in it), then the loan will remain unregulated.

Why SPVs are OK

- If you recognised the acronym, then you're most likely in or want to get into the Buy To Let sector of mortgage lending. The sectors doing OK, especially with landlord clients buying through a limited company or better known as an SPV – Special Purpose Vehicle.

- An SPV is essentially a limited company set up purely to buy, manage and rent residential properties. It owns the properties in the portfolio, and the business is run by directors.

- This week I've been working with lender's teams, and we've been discovering the benefits of buying property via an SPV:

  - If you're a higher rate taxpayer, you're going to lose your high rate tax relief on your mortgage interest if you buy alone, that could mean making a loss. Buying through an SPV means you receive full relief against mortgage interest on your Corporation Tax. Plus relief on everything else you spend on the letting business.

  - There's plenty of great mortgage deals for SPVs – on par now with borrowing individually.

  - The rental coverage is more generous for SPVs – this means that you can borrow more money on a stated amount of rent.

  - You can bring in a non-earning spouse to reduce tax.

  - Setting up an SPV is cheap and quick – only costs £12 and can be done in 30 minutes.

  - The taxation advantages continue with the ability to take income from the SPV and pay a lower dividend tax rate.

- Of course, your client must talk to their accountant – I mean who wouldn't, and there are some drawbacks, but as a professional mortgage broker, you should be able to hold a conversation on the topic with confidence.

Deferred Mortgages

- Relatively popular in the early 1990's when interest rates hit a peak of 15.4%. They were designed to assist the borrower to keep down costs in the early years, often by deferring capital repayments during a specified initial period.

- Unpaid interest was added to the outstanding capital balance.

- A deferred mortgage differed in that the deferred interest was the same amount for an initial set period. The jump at the end of the deferred period was dramatic.

- Attractive to those who want to maximise the loan and minimise the repayments in the early years.

- Borrowers must be relatively sure of having an increasing income, although in reality they were sold to many people.

Sharia or Islamic Mortgages

- Also known as Home Purchase Plans.
- Muslims are not allowed to pay interest on a loan, so conventional mortgages would not be suitable.
- There are two types – the Ijara and the Murabaha.
- Both are now regulated mortgage loans.

Ijara Mortgage

- This involves the lender buying the property from the vendor and paying Stamp Duty.
- The applicants repay the purchase price in instalments over the term.
- Every month a rent is paid also which replaces interest.
- At the end of the term, the lender transfers the house to the applicants who become owners.

Murabaha

- The difference is that once the lender has bought the property, they sell it straight to the applicants at a higher price.
- This higher price which reflects lost interest payments is repaid in equal instalments over the term, with an initial payment of 20%

Sub Prime and Non-Status Mortgages

Sub Prime Mortgages

- Certain lenders have carved themselves a niche in the subprime area of lending.
- In a nutshell, someone with a bad credit risk can obtain mortgage finance via a sub-prime mortgage.
- These loans take into account borrower's credit history and charge slightly higher interest rates to reflect the extra risk.
- Arrangement fees tend to be higher as is the procuration fee paid to brokers and larger deposits are often needed by borrowers.
- Many High Street lenders have created subsidiary lenders who carry out the sub-prime work for the lender.

Non-Status or Self-Certified Mortgages

- MCOB rules state that lenders must ensure that loans are affordable by each borrower, and this has ensured that the non-status mortgage market has declined.
- What remains though are self-certified loans, where legitimate income is put into the application, but the lender doesn't verify this income.
- These can be useful for people who have income but can't prove or validate it.
- Higher deposits are normally the order of the day accompanied by arrangement fees and slightly higher interest rates.
- Unfortunately, in the past, fraudulent claims of higher income have been made to obtain a bigger mortgage than would normally be advanced.
- These mortgages have since been banned by the FCA, but existing customers may still have them.

HomeBuy Schemes

- Began in 2006 and aimed to allow 100,000 households to buy their own property in areas where they would not normally be able to afford.

- Also known as the key workers scheme, the basic principle is equity share.

- Aimed at three groups:
  - Social tenants and those on the housing register.
  - Key workers in the health service, education, and safety sector.
  - Priority first-time buyers who can't afford their own home.

- There were a number of schemes devised since 2006 – First Buy, HomeBuy Direct, My Choice and Own Home – and they worked on the basis of sharing the equity to reduce the cost.

- These have all been outdated and phased out with the advent of the popular Help to Buy Equity Loan Scheme.

- The one remaining scheme is the NewBuy which provides a government indemnity to secure a mortgage of 95% on a new build below a purchase price of £500,000.

"Replaced by robots... what can they do that we can't?"

Help to Buy

Equity Loan Scheme

- Since April 2013 the scheme has made it possible to borrow up to 20% of the cost of a new build from the government.

- You only need a 5% deposit and a 75% mortgage to make up the rest.

- Available in England for affiliated new builds with a value up to £600,000.

- Both first-time buyers and existing homeowners are eligible.

- Buyers need a minimum deposit of 5%.

- You must occupy the property, and it must be your only property.

- With the Equity Loan scheme, you can borrow 20% of the purchase price of a new build property valued up to £600,000.

- You won't have to pay anything on the 20% loan for the first five years. In the sixth year, you will be charged 1.75% of the loan's value, which will increase every year by the retail price index plus 1%.

- Developers must take part in the Equity Loan scheme to qualify

Mortgage Guarantee Scheme

- The Mortgage Guarantee scheme makes it possible to purchase a pre-owned or new build property under £600,000 with a 5% deposit.

- Available for pre-owned properties and new builds across the UK - up to the value of £600,000.

- Both existing homeowners and first-time buyers were eligible.

- Buyers needed a minimum of a 5% deposit.

- Closed for new applications in 2016 since the mortgage market readily supplies 95% lending once again.

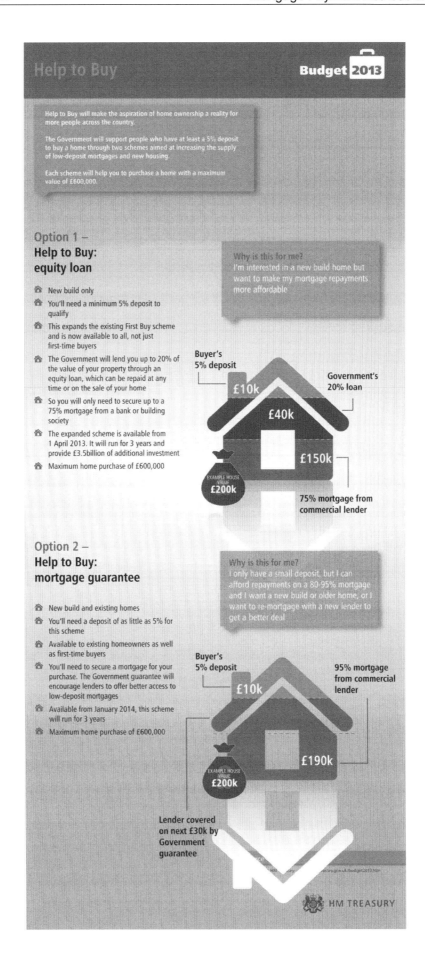

Shared Ownership Mortgage

- This effectively combines rental with owner-occupation.
- The system is used extensively by housing associations and enables people on lower incomes to progressively become owner-occupiers.
- A borrower purchases a certain "stake" (often 25% or 50%) in a property with the aid of a mortgage loan, whilst renting the remainder.
- The borrower has the option to buy further stakes later, thereby reducing the rental element.
- This process of increasing one's stake is known as "staircasing".

Foreign Currency Mortgages

- The amount borrowed is denominated in a foreign currency.

- If the value of sterling declines against the currency in which the mortgage is denominated, the capital outstanding increases (and vice versa).

- They are not suitable for the risk-averse borrower.

- They can be an appropriate borrowing medium for those people whose income is received in the foreign currency in which they borrow.

"I'LL TELL YOU HOW SMART YOUR PORTFOLIO IS, RIGHT NOW IT'S VACATIONING IN SOUTHERN FRANCE."

100% Mortgages

- Many first time buyers struggle to get a foot on the housing ladder.

- The costs of buying property are very high, especially if you exceed the £250,000 bracket for 3% stamp duty.

- To assist these people, lenders make available mortgaged which advance more than the actual purchase price.

- HLCs can be added to the loan.

- Technically not all the loan can be secured as a first charge, so the excess is normally arranged on an unsecured basis but with normal mortgage interest rates.

- The credit crunch has put paid to all 100% mortgages, and maximum loan to values have been reduced across the board to 80% to 90%.

Commercial Mortgages

- Commercial mortgages can be used for a variety of purposes, such as:
    - the purchase of business premises ;
    - extension of existing premises;
    - residential and commercial investment;
    - property development;
- Most banks and building societies offer commercial mortgages.
- Deposits are usually required.
- A commercial lender will expect your business to be stable and profitable. They may ask to see the business plan and long-term financial projections, to assure themselves that your business has, and will continue to have, the ability to make repayments on the loan.
- Some lenders impose restrictions on the uses of commercial premises, and certain business concerns may be excluded altogether.
- The interest rate is typically, it will be between 1 per cent and 6 per cent above the Bank of England base rate. But they are negotiable.
- There are two interest rate options - variable or fixed. In addition, capital and interest or interests only are available.
- Fees
    - Arrangement or processing fees. A typical fee might be in the region of 0.5-1.5 per cent of the loan and is usually negotiable.
    - Valuation fee.
    - Redemption penalty .
- Minimum level for the loan - commercial mortgages are usually only given for substantial amounts, ranging from £15,000 to over £1 million, with higher sums in other circumstances depending on the value of your property and the nature of your business.
- Personal guarantee – the bank may ask you for a personal guarantee as additional security, especially for high percentage loans.
- National Association of Commercial Finance Brokers has a code of practice for selling commercial loans.

Releasing Equity

Home Income Plans

- The client(s) take a loan secured on their home.
- They use the loan to buy a purchased life annuity providing income for life (or until the second death in the case of couples).
- Part of the annuity income is used to pay the interest on the loan.
- Interest relief given on loans to purchase certain life annuities (home income plans) in existence on 9 March 1999 that still qualify for relief, is fixed at 23% for the first £30,000 of the loan from 6 April 2000.
- On death (or second death of a couple) the loan is repaid from the proceeds of the sale of the house.
- In the meantime, the owners agree to maintain and repair the property.
- Any increase in the value of the property between affecting the plan and death accrues to the estate of the deceased.

Lifetime Mortgages

- No capital or repayments are required during the life of the mortgage.
- Interest accrues and is rolled up and added to the debt.
- The loan is paid in the event of the borrower's death or if they choose to move.
- Maximum lending is normally 25% to 55% of the value, depending on the borrower's age.
- Lenders operate a no negative equity guarantee.

Shared Appreciation Mortgages

- Mainly phased out now but worth knowing about.

- An elderly homeowner, in dire need of cash, takes out a mortgage on their home.

- The lender makes no interest charge or a very small percentage.

- The lender takes a percentage share of any *increase* in the value of the property in return for no or low interest.

Home Reversion Schemes

- The company takes over ownership of the property but permits the former owner to remain in occupation until death, or second death of a couple (who in turn agree to keep the property in good repair).

- In exchange, the company pays a lump sum (less than the current value of the property) or an income for life.

- In general, these arrangements produce more cash for the owners, but they lose ownership of their property.

- A leaseback arrangement is set up allowing the previous owner to stay in the property in return for a nominal ground rent.

- No interest is paid by the previous owner and the amount of money given reflects this.

- Capital can be used for any purpose or used to buy an annuity.

- Once the previous owner dies for moves into care, the property is sold, and the plan provider received their share percentage of the property with the remainder falling into the estate of the previous owners.

"You'll never get a mortgage!"

Equity Release Council

- Safe Home Income Plans (SHIP) was launched in 1991 as a result of a collective initiative by the main providers of Home Income Plans.

- Renamed the Equity Release Council

- Companies subscribing to the Code of Practice undertake to provide a fair, simple and complete presentation of any home income plan they may offer you.

- The Code has been welcomed by Age Concern.

  - You will be given full details of your own obligations, commitments and rights under the plan, including security of tenure on your home for you and your partner for the rest of your lives.

  - You will be told what costs are involved, your tax position and the possible effect on your plan of moving house and of changing house values, as well as the effect of the transaction on the value of your estate on death.

  - Your own solicitors will act on your behalf and look after your interests at every stage. Before your scheme can be finalised, they will be required to sign a certificate confirming the principal terms of the contract and confirming that they have been fully explained to you.

  - An Equity Release Council plan guarantees that you cannot lose your home – whatever happens to the stock market or to interest rates.

Mortgage Payment Protection Insurance (MPPI)

- Also known as ASU – Accident, Sickness and Unemployment.
- These are general insurance (not life assurance) products.
- Typically, the policy:
  - Is renewable annually (i.e. not a long-term policy such as PHI - see below);
  - Provides benefits for a maximum of two years;
  - Has a short waiting period/deferred period after the event before benefit payment commences, typically 28 days.
  - Does not cover loss of earnings for self-employed people;
  - No requirement for a medical.
  - Tax-free.

"I CUT MYSELF SHAVING."

Income Protection Insurance

- IPI provides an income during disability caused by sickness or injury. It is available to employees and the self-employed.

- 'Permanent' means that the policy cannot be cancelled by the company.

- Deferred period (usually 4, 13, 26, 52 weeks) must elapse from start of disability before benefits begin.

- Benefits are then paid until recovery, retirement or death.

- Disability is defined in terms of being unable to work (a typical definition might be: unable to follow own occupation or any other for which suited by training/experience).
  - Some companies offer limited benefits to housewives.
  - Proportionate benefit may be payable if a lower-paid job is taken due to disability.

- Maximum benefit usually 60% to 65% of income, plus state incapacity benefits.

- Protection is for a chosen term ending at or before state retirement age.

- Premium levels are higher for some occupations

- Policies can be pure protection, or on a unit-linked basis, Benefits are tax-free for policies effected by individuals.

- Types of premiums
  - Reviewable – increase over the term
  - Renewable – renewed periodically according to market risks at the time
  - Guaranteed – remain the same

Taxation

- Individual plans are tax-free

- Company sponsored plans are taxable when the employee receives the income, but most are not treated as a benefit in kind although they are charged as a tax-deductible business expense.

ASU 2 - IPI 3

- Accident, sickness and Unemployment insurance has had a bad rap since the PPI scandal took hold. Payment Protection Insurance is essentially the same type of policy but can be used to cover any debt. Hence many people with credit cards have claimed for mis-selling PPI.

  - ASU and IPI – Income Protection Insurance are very different.
  - ASU covers just the mortgage payment plus associated insurances; IPI covers the salary.
  - ASU typically protects for up to two years; IPI can cover until retirement, mine takes me to age 70
  - ASU has a standard deferred period of one month before payments are made; IPI has options where the customer can choose – anything up to a year
  - ASU covers in the event of redundancy from employment but has plenty of caveats – the customer mustn't have known of any impending redundancy before they took out the plan, and usually, they need to have a period of full employment before claiming. Plus they impose a period when the plan starts, where no customer can claim at all.
  - ASU are general insurance policies, so they renew each year just like motor. IPI is permanent.
  - ASU benefits are tax-free just like IPI, and both don't allow tax relief on premiums like pensions. They are the same when employers take them out for their staff — the costs are offset against Corporation Tax for both plans.

- So it's ASU 2 – IPI 5!

Critical Illness Cover

- In addition to as opposed to being required instead of IPI.

- This policy provides a lump sum benefit in the event of the life assured being diagnosed as suffering from any one of a number of designated illnesses or conditions, or requiring certain specified treatments. These typically include:

  - Heart attack;
  - Heart bypass surgery;
  - Cancer;
  - Kidney disease;
  - Stroke.

- Such illnesses can cause as much, if not more, financial difficulty as can death.

- The policy benefit could be used to:

  - Pay off a mortgage or other loans;
  - Fund the adaptation of the property to meet medical needs - such as wheelchair access;
  - Pay for private medical treatment or nursing.

"THAT'S YOUR SUGGESTION DOBBS? A FREE CASKET WITH EVERY POLICY?"

Annual Percentage Rate (APR)

- Introduced by Consumer Credit Act 1974.
- Intended to be a means of comparing the overall cost of credit - including any fees and charges as well as the interest and repayments.
- It must be quoted by lenders whenever the published rate of interest is used in advertisements and marketing.
- It is based on a number of assumptions, including:
  - The interest rate remains unchanged throughout the loan;
  - The mortgage term is uninterrupted, and all payments are made on time;
  - No life assurance premiums are allowed for;
  - No tax relief is claimable (i.e. it is a gross rate);
  - Early redemption will not occur;
- Various items are excluded from the calculation:
  - Default charges;
  - Fines;
  - Redemption interest;
  - Endowment premiums;
- These assumptions and restrictions make APR a relatively meaningless figure in all but the simplest cases, and almost totally meaningless for endowment and pension mortgages.

Annual Percentage Rate of Charge (APRC)

- The APRC (Annual Percentage Rate of Charge) is the total cost of the credit to the consumer, expressed as an annual percentage.

- You can use this to compare quotes from different lenders as they all have to calculate the APRC in exactly the same way.

- The calculation assumes that you keep your mortgage product and provider for the entire term and that the rates shown do not change even if the rate is described as variable.

Example Calculation

- Example input values:
    - Loan Amount: £125,000
    - Term: 25 years
    - Initial Rate: 3.5% (fixed)
    - Initial Term: 2 years
    - Subsequent Rate: 5.5% (variable)
    - Lender fees: £999
- Repayment example
    - The total amount repayable is £225,131.92 (This value takes into account the fees, the interest rates and the term).
    - This means that you would pay back £1.80 for every £1 borrowed. The APRC is 5.3%.

Interest Rate Volatility

- Below is a chart and graph which shows interest rate movements over the last decade.

	Standard Variable Rate *	Typical Fixed Rate **	RPI
1997	7.00%	6.75%	3.10%
1998	7.50%	6.75%	3.40%
1999	6.75%	6.75%	1.50%
2000	8.00%	6.50%	3.00%
2001	6.00%	6.50%	1.80%
2002	5.00%	6.50%	1.70%
2003	6.00%	6.50%	2.90%
2004	6.00%	5.75%	3.00%
2005	6.50%	5.75%	2.80%
2006	5.50%	5.75%	3.20%
2007	6.50%	5.75%	3.75%
2008	7.00%	6.50%	0.50%
2009	5.00%	3.50%	2.00%
2010	5.00%	4.00%	4.10%
2011	4.75%	3.50%	4.10%
2012	4.00%	3.50%	2.50%
2013	4.00%	3.00%	3.30%

*   Hanley Economic Building Society
** 5 Year

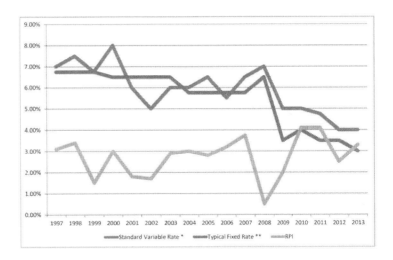

- The RPI obviously affects the interest rates. You can see that the RPI moves, then the interest rate moves with it.

- If you look at the beginning of each fixed period, you'd notice that it was quite competitive with the variable rate, just slightly below. This is because these need to be attractive with the additional advantage of being able to budget over the period.

- Between 2001 and 2004, the variable rate was more competitive.

Interest Rests

Annual rests

- Annual interest is debited to the account at the start of the financial year.
- Repayments are set against it (normally monthly).
- If the mortgage is redeemed during the year, the account is adjusted with the appropriate number of days' interest.
- The method does not penalise late payers or reward early payers.

Monthly rests

- Credit Cards typically use this method
- Interest is debited to the account on a monthly basis.
- Repayments are set against it, also normally monthly. In most cases, the borrower effectively pays interest as it falls due.

Daily Rest

- Much more common these days with the popularity of flexible mortgages.
- Interest is calculated and added to the outstanding loan on a daily basis.
- It is simple to run with the help of computers.
- This rewards early payers and penalises those delay making repayments.

Annual review schemes

- Some lenders permit borrowers to fix the repayment amount for a year at a time to simplify borrowers' financial planning.
- Note that this does not affect the interest *due*, which could increase and leave the borrower with an increased debt.

Mortgage Products Summary

CeMAP Mainstream Products

Product Description	Product
This product has the interest rate linked to an external interest rate and not the lender's normal variable rate. The rate is set by the Bank of England each month.	Base Rate Tracker
This mortgage has a normal variable interest rate charged but has a maximum rate and a minimum rate of interest.	Cap & Collar
This product involves you having a mortgage at the normal variable rate and to make things more comfortable, the lender gives you a large sum of money up front, all for free.	Cashback
This product allows a reduction in the normal mortgage rate over a period of time. This reduction is a gift and is not repaid at all. Often the reduction only lasts for a period of time.	Discounted Rate
This is where the interest rate remains the same throughout a specified term of years.	Fixed Rate
This mortgage allows you to make variable payments on your mortgage. Make overpayments, underpayments and even take payment holidays.	Flexible
This involves a mortgage-free property where the owner wishes to raise a lump sum. They, therefore, affect a mortgage on their property and use the money raised as their lump sum. Normal monthly repayments are made which ensure the outstanding loan either reduces or remains the same.	Home Income Plan

Product Description	Product
A situation where we have an elderly person or people living in their mortgage free property and they wish to raise a lump sum. Here a company steps in to take over some ownership of the property, maybe 50%, and give the owner a lump sum of money in return. They live there until their death when the company then claims its ownership of the property.	Home Reversionary
This product has the interest rate linked to an external interest rate and not the lender's normal variable rate. This external rate is often quoted in the press as the most up to date rate of interest in the UK.	LIBOR Tracker
This mortgage allows you to link the loan to a deposit account or current account you have with the same lender. So when you have your interest calculated each month on your outstanding debt, the credit balances from your other accounts are used to reduce the debt, so you pay less interest. The more money you have in your deposit accounts, the lower your monthly payment.	Off Set
This is the standard mortgage product, and it is where the interest rate charged varies according to the lenders normal mortgage rate. It is usually the rate that accounts revert to after a fixed, capped or discount product ends.	Variable Rate

Mortgage Payment Methods & Products

Variable Rate	
Positive Features	Negative Features
• Benefit from falling interest rates • Always have lender's current rate which is going to be market competitive • No arrangement or redemption penalties	• Suffer when interest rates increase

Base Rate Tracker	
Positive Features	Negative Features
• Benefit from falling interest rates • Always competitive because it's linked to the Bank of England Base Rate • No arrangement or redemption penalties	• Suffer when interest rates increase

LIBOR Tracker	
Positive Features	Negative Features
• Benefit from falling interest rates quicker than other products • Always competitive because it's linked to the LIBOR • No arrangement or redemption penalties	• Suffer when interest rates increase • Usually only available for commercial mortgages

Fixed Rate	
Positive Features	Negative Features
• No increase in payments when interest rates increase	• No benefit when rates fall • Usually large arrangement fees and redemption penalties • Reverts to the normal variable rate after term which might cause a shock

Discounted Rate	
Positive Features	Negative Features
• Useful reduction in interest rates for a period of time • No need to repay the discount back to the lender • Benefit from falling interest rates	• Suffer when interest rates increase • Sometimes there might be arrangement fees or redemption penalties

Cap and Collar	
Positive Features	Negative Features
• No increase in payments when interest rates increase above capped rate • Falling interest rates will reduce your own rate subject to the limit placed by the collar	• Usually large arrangement fees and redemption penalties • Reverts to the normal variable rate after term which might cause a shock

Cashback

Positive Features	Negative Features
• Large cash lump sum available at outset • No need to repay this cash sum	• Redemption penalties, i.e. repayment of cash within set term • Usually, normal variable rate or tracker rates so no discounts available.

Home Income Plan

Positive Features	Negative Features
• Ability to raise lump sum for any purpose. • You know up front how much the debt is going to be against property	• Need to pay monthly mortgage payments unless lifetime mortgage opted for. which requires no payments, just roll up of capital. • Less equity in property to pass in your Will

Home Reversionary Plan

Positive Features	Negative Features
• Large lump sum available to use for any purpose • No monthly payments to make	• Some of your equity will pass onto someone else on your death • The amount of equity will be unknown as it is usually a percentage of the current value

Flexible	
Positive Features	Negative Features
• Ability to underpay and overpay repayments • Payment holiday feature • Benefit from lump sum repayments • Benefit from falling interest rates	• Rising interest rates will affect your mortgage payments

Off Set	
Positive Features	Negative Features
• One monthly payment to cover a variety of savings and loan accounts. • Other loans benefit from the lower mortgage rate • All your accounts under one roof	• Have to have all savings and loans with one lender

CeMAP Other Products

Product Description	Product
This mortgage, rather than taking your salary into account uses the expected rent from a tenant to support the mortgage payments.	Buy To Let
These mortgages are arranged non-sterling currencies. All mortgage payments must be made in that currency, and the outstanding debt is denominated in the same currency.	Foreign currency
This involves a mortgage-free property where the owner wishes to raise a lump sum. They, therefore, affect a mortgage on their property and use the money raised as their lump sum. No monthly payments are made, so the outstanding debt rolls up until the property is sold.	Lifetime
These mortgages, not available any more, allow you to pay a lower monthly mortgage payment than would otherwise be charged. This underpayment has to be paid back at some stage and is usually accumulated and added to the loan after a set period of years.	Deferred
A mortgage designed to allow a tenant to buy their home from the local authority or housing association usually at a substantial discount to the market value.	Right to Buy
This mortgage advances the money in instalments over a period of time whilst you're building your house.	Self-build
These mortgages allow you to buy a half (or similar) share of a property now and rent the remainder from the housing association. Staircasing allows you to purchase further shares of the property over time.	Shared ownership
This mortgage is based on the concept that you are not allowed to pay or receive interest. Instead, the lender buys the property and lets you live in it whilst you make instalments. When these have been paid, the house is yours.	Sharia

Product Description	Product
This mortgage is designed for someone who doesn't have a perfect bill of health when it comes to their credit rating. Usually charged at a higher rate of interest	Sub Prime

Lifetime

Positive Features	Negative Features
• Ability to raise a substantial lump sum • No burden of monthly repayments	• As no repayments made at all, unpaid interest will roll up and increase the amount outstanding; this will eat into the equity

Deferred

Positive Features	Negative Features
• Higher multiples means you can borrow more • Much lower monthly repayments in the early years. 2% or 3% reduction were common	• Can't buy them any more • Unpaid interest is added to the mortgage after the low start term meaning massive increase in debt. • Interest rate will increase after low start term, meaning monthly payments will increase.

Self Build

Positive Features	Negative Features
• Allows the mortgage to be fed to the client in stages so they can self fund their own build project	• Funds are released once certain build stages have been completed so the client will have to wait a certain time before the money is released

Foreign Currency

Positive Features	Negative Features
• By borrowing in another currency, you might benefit from lower interest rates.	• Currency fluctuations could cause both your mortgage payments and outstanding loan to increase dramatically

Buy To Let

Positive Features	Negative Features
• Allows the lender to look at your potential rental income in deciding how much to lend, rather than your personal income	• Usually, a large deposit is needed • Interest rates possibly slightly higher than variable rate although competition ensures you get a favourable rate.

Right to Buy

Positive Features	Negative Features
• Mortgage that enables council tenants to buy their homes with a substantial discount • Additional borrowing to fund improvements	• Council have a clawback clause which means that you have to repay the discount if you move in the early years

Mortgage Payment Methods & Products

Shared Ownership

Positive Features	Negative Features
• Allows you to buy a share of a property from a housing association and rent the remainder, thus keeping your costs down • Normally allows "Staircasing" which benefits you by being able to borrow additional sums to purchase extra shares of the property, eventually owning the whole property	• Rent needs to be paid on the un-owned portion • The property usually has to be sold back to the housing association or to someone on their list

Sub Prime

Positive Features	Negative Features
• Allows people who have experienced financial problems in the past to obtain a mortgage, who otherwise would struggle to be considered	• Higher rates of interest generally • Often large fees involved which are added to the loan • Arrears procedures are harsh if they do miss any payments

Self Certificated

Positive Features	Negative Features
• Allows people who cannot prove their income to obtain a mortgage they need • Very quick process	• Not always the most competitive mortgage rates • No longer allowed • Usually, a large deposit is required typically 20% so not for first-time buyers

Sharia	
Positive Features	Negative Features
• Allows people whose customs do not allow them to pay interest, to obtain a mortgage	• The ownership of the property remains with the lender until repayments are completed

A Repayment Vehicle MOT

	With profit Endowment	Low Cost With profit Endowment	Unit Linked Endowment	Pension policy	Equity ISA
Flexible Premium	No	No	Yes	Yes	Yes
Fixed Term	Yes	Yes	No	No specific term	No
Life Cover Included	Yes	Yes	Yes	No	No
Cash in early	Penalties for surrendering early	Penalties for surrendering early	Yes	No	Yes
Tax	Basic rate tax is paid for within the fund. At the end of the term, the proceeds are paid tax-free so long as the policy remains qualifying	Basic rate tax is paid for within the fund. At the end of the term, the proceeds are paid tax-free so long as the policy remains qualifying	Basic rate tax is paid for within the fund. At the end of the term, the proceeds are paid tax-free so long as the policy remains qualifying	Contributions attract tax relief at the client's highest rate of tax. 25% lump sum is tax-free	Investors exempt from CGT and income tax
Benefits	Guarantee that mortgage will be cleared on maturity or death. Any bonuses added will provide a surplus at the end of the term.	Guarantee that mortgage will be cleared on death.	Potential to achieve greater gains or repay mortgage early. Guarantee that mortgage will be cleared on death. Control over the particular type of investments	Tax advantages of investment growth and proceeds	Tax advantages
Drawbacks	Expensive	No guarantee that maturity figure would be enough to repay your mortgage. It could leave you with a deficit when your mortgage has to be repaid.	No guaranteed sum assured at maturity; therefore no guarantee that maturity figure would be enough to repay your mortgage.	The 25% tax-free lump sum may not be adequate to clear the outstanding balance on your mortgage. Have to arrange separate life cover	Max investment is £20,000 per annum. Have to arrange separate life cover

4 Post Completion

Further advances

Consumer Credit Act 2006

- Loans to personal borrowers are regulated by the Act unless they are exempt.
- They are exempt if:
  - They are for the purchase, improvement, enlargement, alteration or repair of a main dwelling house; and
  - The original loan was with the same lender.
  - If a loan is for mixed purposes, it is separated into regulated and non-regulated elements, and the two parts separately dealt with.
- Key points:
  - Establishing an ombudsman facility – the Financial Services Ombudsman Service.
  - Allowing challenging of unfair lending practices.
  - Improving the quality of information.
  - Removal of the £25,000 cap from previous legislation.
  - Business loans excluded, but self-employed and partnership loans will be included.
  - Regulation of the Consumer Credit Act was transferred from the Office of Fair Trading (OFT) to the FCA on 1st April 2014

Assessment of status

- Personal and family circumstances.
    - May have changed since the original loan.
    - If new people have moved in, "consent to mortgage" forms required.
- Outgoings.
    - Comprehensive details of regular and irregular expenditure.
    - Including other borrowings.
- Conduct of existing account.
    - Indicates quality of payment record etc.
    - Any arrears would have to be cleared before a further loan is considered.

Assessment of security

- Value of property
    - Value may have increased or decreased.
    - If original loan-to-value ratio was high, another valuation may be required.
- If the loan is for home improvements, the lender may base loan on an estimate of the value after alterations.
- Loan required
    - The overall loan-to-value ratio is the important factor here.
    - i.e. outstanding original loan plus new loan, in proportion to value.
- Location
    - The neighbourhood may have changed as a result of (for example):
    - New major roads nearby, building of factories, schools, prison etc.
- Purpose of the loan
    - If the loan is for improvements or extensions, they must be consistent with planning regulations.
- The risk decision
    - As with all loan applications, the lender has to balance the need to obtain business, and the possibility of cross sales of related business, against the need to lend within acceptable risk parameters.
    - A loan to an existing customer on the security of a known property offers easier opportunities to assess some of the risk factors.

Postponement of second charge

- A second charge is a right over a mortgaged property exercised by a lender subsequent to the first mortgagee.

- Priority of mortgages is determined in England and Wales by the Law of Property Act 1925 and broadly speaking priority is in chronological order.

- If a lender has a first charge and wishes to take a third charge, with a different lender having a second charge, the first lender may persuade the other lender to postpone its prior charge in favour of a new one (by a deed of postponement).

- The process of adding a subsequent mortgage to an original one, having postponed an intervening one, is known as *tacking*.

Planning Permission

- Further advances for home improvements must be subject to the borrower obtaining all the necessary planning consents.

Listed Buildings

- These need additional consent for any alterations or improvements.

- National Heritage give this permission in a similar way to applying for planning permission

Architect's Certificates

- Required if a member of NHBC is not carrying out the work.

- Usually appropriate for large extensions or new build.

Lender Assistance with Arrears

Re-schedule repayments

- Clear the arrears by paying an increased amount for a specified period. Known as an arrangement.//
- Lenders normally want the period over which borrowers get up to date to be relatively short (6 to 12 months).
- Under the Administration of Justice Act 1973, courts have the power to determine a longer period, often set at one to four years.
- However, the case of *Cheltenham & Gloucester v. Morgan* appears to have set a precedent for arrears to be spread over the full remaining mortgage period.
- Some forms of debt/budget counselling may be available from the lender or through outside professionals.

Accept interest only

- A possible method on repayment mortgages only.

Extend the term

- If a person owes a few months' arrears, the lender may extend the term of the mortgage by that same period.
- Can be used for repayment mortgages.
- May not be possible with an endowment mortgage, as the repayment vehicle has a fixed term. Other interest only methods may be more flexible.

Other actions

- Surrendering the endowment policy (not generally recommended as the return may be small in relation to premiums paid).
- Trading down to a smaller property.

Arrangements

- An arrangement is a formal term used to describe when a borrower and a lender have come to an agreement on repaying the outstanding arrears with extra monthly payments.

- It usually takes the form of an agreement between lender and borrower to spread the payment of arrears over a specified period.

- Arrangements should be:
  - Confirmed in writing by the lender;
  - Monitored to check that the borrower is carrying out the agreement;
  - Followed up in writing if the borrower fails to meet his obligations under the agreement.

- Reasons for this are:
  - To ensure that, if the lender has to go to court to recover a debt or to take possession of a property, it can be clearly shown everything has been done to try to help the borrower.
  - The courts have extensive powers, under the Administration of Justice Acts 1970 and 1973 (Conveyancing and Feudal Reform Act 1970, in Scotland), to halt or suspend the processes of taking possession if it appears that the borrower could eventually work off the arrears.
  - To maintain the records necessary to make provision for anticipated losses.

"WHICH HALF WOULD YOU LIKE? THE CAR DEBT OR THE HOUSE DEBT?"

Government Support for Arrears and Repossessions

Support for Mortgage Interest (SMI)

- Support for Mortgage Interest (SMI), pays the interest on mortgages up to £200,000 of a loan or mortgage. If you're getting Pension Credit, this figure is £100,000.

- The receipt of SMI is now configured as a secured loan, secured as a second charge on your property and repaid on sale. The interest payable is currently 1.5%

- SMI is normally paid directly to the lender after a waiting period, which is 39 weeks

- Where the borrower is receiving Pension Credit, there's no waiting period.

- The standard interest rate is used to calculate SMI, currently 2.61%

- What's not included:
  - capital - only the interest is paid
  - anything towards insurance policies
  - arrears

- Run-on - Once you start a job that will last 5 weeks you will receive 4-week "run-on."

- 52 Week Rule – if you start work and fall out of work within 52 weeks, there is no need to serve another 13 week wait period.

Mortgage Rescue Scheme

- Helps borrowers facing repossession and offered by local authorities.
- A shared equity loan offered to reduce costs.
- Government mortgage to rent, i.e. housing association buys property and lets the person rent it.
- Only available where no other option available to borrow.
- Income of less than £60,000.

Taking Possession

- The lender petitions the county court for a possession order.
- The court will seek to be satisfied that every other possible avenue has been explored and that possession is the last resort.
- The court can take one of three actions. It could grant:
  - Outright possession - the lender can take possession within 28 days;
  - Suspended possession - directs the borrower to make specified payments, with the lender able to take possession if he fails to do so;
  - Adjournment until a specified date.
- Having taken possession, the lender can require the borrower to vacate the premises. Locks should be changed and any other steps taken to ensure that the borrower cannot re-enter the premises. Utilities may have to be disconnected. Suppliers should be informed, and meters read.
- Any fittings left behind are held on trust for the mortgagor, and if not reclaimed within a certain time should be sold and the proceeds credited to the mortgage account.
- The lender can then sell the property, although the borrower has the right to settle the mortgage account at any time before the property is sold.

Selling a Repossessed Property

- Once under possession, the mortgage account has an alarming habit of increasing out of control, so the lender has the duty to obtain the best price in the quickest possible time.

- The placing of newspaper notices seeking final offers by a particular date may prove they have attempted to get the best possible price.

- The borrower retains an equity of redemption (the right to settle the mortgage debt at any time up to sale) even after the lender has taken possession.

- If the lender sells a property but fails to achieve an appropriate selling price, the borrower can sue for damages.

"WE'RE DOWNSIZING, MORRISON. YOU'RE THE FIRST TO SHRINK."

Alternative Remedies

Sue on personal covenant

- The lender attempts to enforce the borrower's contractual obligation, in the legal charge, to repay the debt.
- This is often impossible, as the borrower does not have the resources.

Appoint a receiver

- Applies when there is an income from the property, e.g. there are tenants paying a rent from a buy to let mortgage
- The money is collected and applied to the mortgage account to reduce the debt.

Foreclosure

- Foreclosure is never used today. It would result in the borrower forfeiting all rights to the property (and hence losing any equity).

Repossession Register

- The Possessions Register was set up in August 1991 by the CML and two major credit reference agencies, to record details of mortgage borrowers whose homes have been taken into possession by a lender.

- The main aim of the Register is to prevent fraud, should a borrower try to obtain a mortgage without telling the lender that they had fallen into arrears on a previous mortgage, or had voluntarily surrendered their home.

- The Register holds information on cases where a borrower has voluntarily surrendered their home to the lender, as well as cases where a lender has taken possession of a property with a court order.

- All of this information is submitted by the mortgage lender directly to the credit reference agencies. Borrowers' details are kept on the Register for six years from the date the possession took place.

- The register is operated by two credit reference agencies:
    - Experian
    - Equifax.

"YOU ASKED FOR A LARGER CHECK, EMBREY, SO I'M PAYING YOU EVERY OTHER MONTH."

How is the Debt Chased?

- If the sale proceeds are not enough to pay off the money owing to the lender, the borrower faces a "shortfall debt", which they still owe to the lender after possession.

- The action that the lender will take depends on the circumstances. Usually, the lender will contact the borrower as soon as possible after the sale of the property and give a final financial statement. This will show the level of debt still owing to the lender.

- In England, Wales and Northern Ireland, a lender legally has 12 years in which to contact the borrower to begin the process of obtaining repayment of shortfall debt; this period is usually 5 years in Scotland.

- In addition, from 11 February 2000, lenders who are members of the Council of Mortgage Lenders have agreed voluntarily that they will begin all recovery action for the shortfall within the first six years following the sale of a property in possession.

- Anyone whose property was taken into possession and sold more than six years ago, and who has not been contacted by their lender for recovery of any outstanding debt will not now be asked to pay the shortfall.

Transfers of equity

- We live in a fast moving world where flexibility is the key. Transfers of Equity are the lender's way of allowing people to be added to mortgages and removed.

- In either case, the lender's agreement is required.

- In many cases, the request to remove someone from a contract arises because a couple have become divorced or separated.

- Similarly, the main reason for a party to be added to the contract is that the sole mortgagor has become married or has formed a relationship and the new spouse/partner is to become party to the mortgage.

- If a person is to be removed from the mortgage, the remaining mortgagor's financial circumstances must be examined to see if they could support the loan on their own.

- If possible, it should be ascertained who has been paying the mortgage in the past.

- If the reason is divorce, the remaining borrower's circumstances may be made more difficult by the requirement to pay maintenance.

- If a new mortgagor is being added to the loan, normal status enquiries must be made.

- A guarantor or surety must sanction any change in terms and conditions.

- This is particularly important if the person for whom they are the guarantor is the party who is to be released from the contract.

- The possible need for any change to the policy would have to be considered if a mortgagor were being added or removed.

Transfers of Equity and SDLT

- Tax will need to be paid when all or part of an interest in a property is transferred, and anything of monetary value is given in exchange.

- Known as a 'chargeable consideration' which triggers SDLT

- If the chargeable consideration exceeds the Stamp Duty Land Tax threshold, tax could be due.

- Let's assume we have a property worth £150,000 with a remaining mortgage of £100,000. The owner wishes to transfer a half share of the property to their partner, and their partner agrees to pay cash for half of the equity (£25,000) and take responsibility for half of the outstanding mortgage (£50,000).

- The chargeable consideration would be the cash paid £25,000, plus the debt liability taken on £50,000 – a total of £75,000. Since this figure is below the Stamp Duty Land Tax threshold, there will be no tax to pay.

- A couple marry, and one spouse owns a property worth £600,000 with a £450,000 mortgage outstanding. The property is transferred into joint names, and the new spouse takes on half of the mortgage (£225,000).

- The chargeable consideration is the liability that the spouse takes on for the mortgage, and that is the amount (£225,000) on which SDLT is due. Since that figure is above the threshold, tax will be payable, in this case, 2% between £125,000 and £225,000 – a bill of £2,000.

Early redemption

- Reasons for early redemption include:
  - Borrower has received a legacy or other capital receipt, and wishes to pay off obligations;
  - Borrower decides that repaying mortgage would be better than his existing investments;
  - Borrower wishes to move and take a new mortgage with the same or other lender;
  - Borrower wishes to re-mortgage to obtain better terms;
  - Most lenders will attempt to retain the business with attractive offers.

- Early redemption of a mortgage may not be the best use of a lump sum of money. Clients should be encouraged to take an overall view of their financial situation - with independent advice.

- All borrowers have the right to redeem their mortgage before the end of the term.

- The law does not permit lenders to withdraw this right.

- Lenders can charge early redemption fees to offset loss of interest.

- If a court decided that a redemption penalty was so heavy that it effectively prohibited redemption, it could declare it to be a "clog on the equity of redemption" (i.e. it had been imposed deliberately to prevent a borrower from repaying the loan) and could set aside the clause in the conditions or impose a fairer one.

Redemption

- A borrower can be released from his covenants under the terms of a mortgage if the lender is satisfied that all charges to the account have been in full, including:
  - Capital;
  - Interest;
  - Fees, charges and costs.
- The action of the lender in releasing a borrower from his covenants is known as "vacation" of the mortgage.
- A Mortgage Exit Administration Fee (MEAF) would be payable.
- Some lenders permit a nominal debit balance (say of £1) to remain on the mortgage account, as a service to the borrower. This has the effect of:
  - Providing safe custody for the title deeds;
  - Retaining the customer's loyalty with a view to obtaining future business;
  - Allowing borrowers to benefit from conversion to plc status.

Transferring the Mortgage Book

- Normally initiated by lenders who wish to sell all their mortgage business to another lender.
- Can only be done if there is a clause in the legal charge or mortgage conditions permitting it to be done.
- Mortgage transfers are subject to a code of practice.
- Transfers have a number of uses:
  - They can be used to reduce administration of loans in default - by selling the rights to a mortgage for a figure less than the buyer will have the right to collect;
  - They are a way of buying into a particular market or segment;
  - Or alternatively of getting out of a market where margins have been squeezed;
  - They are a way of exchanging an illiquid asset for a liquid one.
- They have some disadvantages:
  - An institution selling its mortgage business (known as its mortgage "book") is unlikely to be able to make a credible return to the marketplace;
  - They may be seen as quick fix for short term financial problems.

Lettings of mortgaged property

- Traditionally lenders were very wary of lending to people who wished to let out their property because:
  - Tenants tend not to treat rented properties with the care they might show for their own property;
  - A tenancy can in certain circumstances become binding on a lender as well as a borrower, making it very difficult to sell a property (e.g. on default).
- However, with the advent of Buy to Let mortgages, lenders are becoming more flexible.
- Mortgage Deed terms and conditions always exclude the borrower's right to let the property without the lender's specific permission.
- The lender will specify:
  - What types of tenancy, if any, are acceptable;
  - Any interest rate change that might apply if the property is let;
  - A requirement to exclude rights of residence that might arise as overriding interests - this will require consent to mortgage form.
- Most lenders will permit letting only in the following circumstances:
  - The letting is for a reasonable purpose;
  - The type of tenancy is acceptable - this normally means an assured shorthold tenancy;
  - That the tenant's right to permanent occupancy are specifically excluded.

Unauthorised Tenancy

- Tenancies can cause lenders problems in the event of repossession, so the trick is to turn a blind eye.

- An unauthorised tenancy confers no rights of occupation, even if rent has been paid.

- Lenders who become aware of an unauthorised tenancy should therefore never acknowledge its existence (e.g. by writing to "the tenant").

- If imposing a new condition, such as a higher interest rate, because the borrower is in breach of the terms and conditions, it must not be implied that the charging of a higher rate sanctions the tenancy.

Other requirements

- Some lenders, when permitting a letting, may require that:
    - The rent is sufficient to cover the mortgage repayment;
    - Bear in mind that income derived from a tenancy is taxable;
    - A professional letting agent must be used to draw up a rental agreement and to collect the rent and deal with other administration.

"A MORTGAGE BURNING PARTY GOT OUT OF HAND!"

Release of part security

- The borrower has a large garden and is approached by a developer to buy some of the land. Not uncommon.
- The borrower wishes to sell part of the mortgaged property, for example:
  - Selling part of a large plot to a developer;
  - Selling to a local authority or highway authority for road widening.

The process

- A plan of the portion to be sold must be drawn.
- The property must be valued to determine whether what remains provides sufficient security for the mortgage.
- If not, a repayment of some of the capital may be required.
- The lender and its Valuer need to take account of the overall longer-term effect of the proposed change. For instance:
  - If land is sold to a property developer, the proximity of a housing development may bring down the value of the remaining property.

Death of a borrower

- Proof of death provided by death certificate - original or photocopy certified by a solicitor.
- Amend records immediately and check for other accounts which the deceased may have had (e.g. savings / investments).
- Avoid issuing inappropriate communications, e.g.:
  - Items addressed to the deceased;
  - Marketing material (especially for life assurance);
  - Attempts to recover arrears within a short time of death.

"FIRST, THE GOOD NEWS IS YOU'LL SOON STOP HAVING COLDS!"

Sole borrower

- The property is vested in the personal representatives of the estate (executors or administrators) who are responsible for the mortgage payments.

- They are responsible for continuing with the obligations under the terms of the mortgage until grant of probate or letters of administration are issued, after which the property may be sold if required, and the mortgage redeemed.

- Once the property is sold, any surplus will be passed on to the estate or to the second mortgagee if applicable.

- The mortgage could be redeemed from the proceeds of a life policy if applicable. If the policy were on a life of another basis or in an appropriate trust, it would not be necessary to wait for probate before redeeming the mortgage.

Joint borrower

- The debt becomes the responsibility of the surviving borrower, who takes on the obligations for the moneys due.

- A life policy may be in place, enabling the mortgage to be redeemed on first death if required.

"IF YOU'LL LEAVE ME YOUR KEYS, DAD — I'D LIKE TO WASH YOUR CAR!"

Bridging finance

- Required when a borrower moves house and can't sell his own property at the same time as buying the new one.
- Instead of breaking the chain, many borrowers choose bridging.

Open bridging

- Buying the new property without having obtained a buyer for the old one. Very high risk for the borrower and for the lender.

Closed bridging

- A buyer has already got a buyer for the property he is moving from.
- Lenders much prefer to lend in closed bridging situations.

Advantages

- Enables purchases to go ahead which might have broken down due to a break in the "chain".

Disadvantages

- Open bridging imposes a high financial burden for an unknown period.
- Bridging is an additional cost at a time when people already have many extra outgoings.
- Bridging can involve a high-interest rate - because of the increased risk to the lender - but not perhaps as high as many people believe.
- Some developers will take properties in part exchange, effectively removing their customers' fear of the possibility of having to resort to bridging finance.

Remortgaging

- A remortgage is a loan that replaces an existing mortgage, either with the existing lender or - more often - with a different lender.

- When the loan is to repay a different lender, most if not all, of the normal considerations for a new loan application, such as:

  ➢ Purpose of the loan;

  ➢ Status and personal circumstances of borrower;

  ➢ Value of the security.

- The present mortgage market makes it extremely easy for people to remortgage and lenders are offering tremendous inducements to encourage people to do so.

Secured Second mortgages

- People who require to release equity for a purpose not related to the property (e.g. buy a car or to finance a business deal) may choose a second mortgage.

- This is an additional loan from a different lender, sitting on top of the original mortgage and secured by a second charge on the property.

- Interest rates are generally higher than the other methods, as the lender's security is less.

- If the borrower defaults on this loan, the property can be sold – the main mortgage would be redeemed first out of the sale proceeds, then the second mortgage.

- Second mortgages are fully regulated under MCOB.

The Joy of Seconds

- Second charge lending only became regulated in 2016 but now forms a good slice of a professional mortgage broker's schemes available to clients.

- We all know what a second charge is, it's a loan secured on property ranked above the first mortgage the client already has in existence. Second charges are easy to arrange, relatively competitively priced and have a flexible underwriting capability.

- So where might you use one for your clients? The two opportunities are raising capital and mortgaging. Instead, consider a second charge because:
  - Second charges are more flexible on maximum ages although many lenders are extending their own maximum ages.
  - Bespoke underwriting, not too much "computer says no."
  - Self-employed applicants are viewed far more flexibly often with just 6 months accounts considered.
  - They can be a good alternative to a further advance for a client who is a "mortgage prisoner" so their existing lender wouldn't be interested.
  - Credit impaired applicants are considered
  - They are much quicker to underwrite
  - They have no need for solicitors as they do all the legal work

- Some compelling reasons to consider adding second charges to your repertoire.

House Insurance Claims

Large claims

- An example of a large claim is subsidence. This would affect the value of the security, so for that reason, the mortgage terms and conditions will allow the lender to control the proceeds of such claims to ensure that the security value is not undermined.

- A lender would only accept a buildings insurance policy if the policy provided the cover which the lender considered necessary.

Empty properties

- Insurance companies may also cancel cover or reduce the level of cover if the borrower is absent for a long period (typically 60 or 90 days).

- If this is likely to happen, lenders need to know in order to take appropriate action to protect their security.

Index-linking

- Most buildings insurances include index linking, which increases the sum insured and premiums.

- Borrowers often feel that the sum insured is too high, but the insurance value may well be different from the property's market value for perfectly valid reasons.

- Sometimes lenders do permit a reduction in insurance value, but this should be accompanied by a requirement for the borrower to indemnify the lender against future losses due to under-insurance.

5 CeMAP 2 Specimen Exam

1. Which one of the following statements regarding a 'second mortgage' is FALSE? Second mortgages:

    a. Are also known as puisne mortgages.

    b. Are secured without deposit of the title deeds.

    c. Represent a higher risk than a first charge.

    d. Usually, have a lower interest rate. ✓

2. Cynthia's mortgage offer contains a disclaimer of the lender's responsibility for the condition of the property. This is to:

    a. Ensure Cynthia obtains a full structural survey of the property.

    b. Ensure the lender is protected from later action by Cynthia. ✓

    c. Protect Cynthia should structural damage subsequently be discovered.

    d. Protect the lender's interest should Cynthia's insurer refuse to pay a claim.

3. Susan has a unit trust mortgage, and Veronica has a low-cost endowment mortgage, what advantage does Susan have over Veronica?

    a. Penalty-free surrender of investment. ✓

    b. Guaranteed loan repayment on death.

    c. Less likelihood of paying CGT.

    d. Lower interest rates for 1st 5 years.

4. Georgina pays a lower rate of interest on part of her mortgage than on the remainder because she has:

   a. A deferred interest mortgage.
   b. A home income plan.
   c. An equity share mortgage.
   d. A shared ownership mortgage.

5. LIBOR related mortgages enable commercial organisations to:

   a. Purchase property at fixed rates of interest.
   b. Take advantage of foreign currency details.
   c. Ensure liquid investment earnings exceed borrowing charges.
   d. Match rates charged with those earned on liquid funds.

6. On the death of a borrower:

   a. The proceeds of any mortgage protection policy will be automatically issued to the lender.
   b. The mortgage account will be closed on production of the Death Certificate.
   c. The lender should register any claim with the personal representative.
   d. Mortgage payments should continue from the borrower's estate.

7. Maggie's home income plan started in 1998 when she took out a £20,000 loan to purchase an annuity. If in the 2019/2020 tax year she is a 68-year-old non-taxpayer, how much tax relief (if any) is she entitled to on the loan interest?

   a. 10%.
   b. 20%.
   c. 23%.
   d. None.

8. At which stage in the house-buying process should a mortgage adviser strongly recommend that any supporting life assurance commence?

   a. When the purchase is agreed.
   b. When the searches are completed.
   c. When contracts are exchanged.
   d. When the purchase is completed.

9. A full with profit endowment mortgage guarantees the borrower:

   a. Repayment of the loan on maturity.
   b. Flexibility regarding the mortgage term.
   c. Payment of a terminal bonus.
   d. Tax efficient low-cost cover.

10. How did the Law of Property Act 1925 affect the rights of a lender?

    a. The lender was no longer deemed to own the property used as security.
    b. The lender was now deemed to own the property if an arrears position arose.
    c. The lender could demand immediate repayment of the loan.
    d. The lender had to apply to the courts in order to take possession of the property.

11. Oliver is interested in a unit-linked endowment mortgage but is concerned about the level of benefit payable on early death. Which of the following can you tell him?

    a. There is no guaranteed minimum payment on death in any circumstances.
    b. The loan is guaranteed to be repaid on death but only if units grow by at least a minimum rate.
    c. Repayment of the loan on death depends on the Policy Review recommendations being followed.
    d. The original loan should always be repaid on death.

12. Mike and Alma both started the same type of mortgage with the same lender on the same day, and both had the same loan-to-value ratio. Why was Alma offered a higher "cashback" than Mike?

    a. Mike's mortgage loan was higher than Alma's
    b. Mike's mortgage loan was lower than Alma's
    c. Mike's mortgage term was longer than Alma's
    d. Mike's mortgage term was shorter than Alma's

13. Guss is purchasing Shane's house. Normally from what date will Guss be responsible for insuring the property?

    a. The date the offer is accepted.
    b. The date contracts are exchanged.
    c. The date completion occurs
    d. The date Guss moves in.

14. Grant has a £80,000 mortgage, £48,000 of which is currently charged at 6% and the balance at 2%. This is because he has a:

   a. Shared ownership mortgage.
   b. Equity Share mortgage.
   c. Fixed mortgage.
   d. Monthly rest mortgage.

15. Which of the following types of search will identify town planning schemes?

   a. Land Registry search.
   b. Parcels Index search.
   c. Local land charges search
   d. Commons registration search.

16. Which statement below is TRUE of unregistered land?

   a. It is not permitted in England and Wales.
   b. Once sold, it will become registered.
   c. It can only be unregistered for another 15 years.
   d. If sold to a public body, it may remain unregistered.

17. How are corporate mortgages dealt with under the Mortgage Conduct of Business Rules?

   a. They are covered up to a maximum of £500,000.
   b. They are wholly excluded.
   c. They are only covered if in excess of £250,000.
   d. They are regulated on a semi-voluntary basis.

18. Dennis is in the process of buying a house and asks his prospective lender to recommend a solicitor. What is considered the best response?

   a. Recommend the first named on the lender's list of approved solicitors.
   b. Recommend the nearest geographically on the lender's shortlist of approved solicitors.
   c. Provide Dennis with a list of solicitors and say he may select one if he considers it appropriate.
   d. Offer to share the services and costs of the lender's solicitor.

19. Larry's house is worth £100,000. His original loan was £60,000 and he requests a further advance of £30,000. If the lender normally requires a HLC for advances in excess of 80%, which statement below applies?

   a. Larry's further advance does not require a HLC.
   b. A HLC will only be required if it was required for the original loan.
   c. A HLC will be required to cover £10,000 of the further advance.
   d. The whole £30,000 should be covered by HLC.

20. In arranging buildings insurance the borrower:

   a. Has complete freedom of choice.
   b. May make his own arrangements subject to the lender's approval.
   c. Will always choose from a panel approved by the lender.
   d. Is obliged to use the lender's provider.

21. If a property is valued at £80,000 and the lender normally offers 80% of the valuation, what mortgage indemnity guarantee would be required for a loan of £70,000?

   a. £6,000.
   b. £10,000.
   c. £14,000.
   d. £16,000.

22. Advice was given on a repayment mortgage on 15 July 2004, and the mortgage commenced on 10 August 2004. How is the administration of the mortgage treated under the Mortgage Conduct of Business Rules?

   a. The regulations do not apply at all.
   b. It is fully regulated.
   c. It is deemed to be semi-regulated.
   d. The transitional regulations apply.

23. If one of two joint tenants dies, the property will automatically:

   a. Belong to the deceased's estate.
   b. Be inherited by any children.
   c. Be held in trust until the death of the survivor.
   d. Belong to the survivor.

24. Bernie has a 20 year £40,000 repayment mortgage with a 2 year fixed rate of 8%. If interest was accounted for on the "annual rest" basis, what is the total debt in his mortgage account on the first day of the mortgage loan?

   a. £40,000.
   b. £40,266.
   c. £43,200.
   d. £46,400.

25. Death benefits during the term of a mortgage-linked low-cost endowment policy consist of three components. What are they?

   a. A with-profits endowment sum assured bonuses plus a decreasing term assurance.
   b. A with-profits endowment sum assured bonuses plus a level term assurance.
   c. A pure endowment sum assured bonuses plus a level term assurance.
   d. A non-profit endowment sum assured, a with profit endowment sum assured plus bonuses.

26. Lionel is self-employed and has submitted his accounts in conjunction with a mortgage application. Which figure is likely to be of MOST interest to his lender?

   a. His monthly drawings of £2,500.
   b. His monthly turnover of £9,500.
   c. His annual net profit of £35,000.
   d. His annual gross profit of £75,000.

27. Why does a low start, low-cost mortgage endowment premium increase by no more than 100% during the increase period?

   a. To ensure reversionary bonuses are maintained throughout the policy.
   b. To obtain tax relief on the premium.
   c. To retain the qualifying status of the policy.
   d. To maintain entitlement to tax relief on capital repayments.

28. When as individual takes out a mortgage, what is used as security for the loan?

   a. An endowment savings plan.
   b. The house being purchased.
   c. The lump sum provided by the mortgagor.
   d. The purchaser's salary

29. In which situation is a closed bridging loan most useful?

   a. Tommy wants to buy his dream house before he can find a buyer for his bungalow.

   b. Tina's vendor wants to complete ahead of her buyer.

   c. Terence wants to build a conservatory but already has a high loan to value.

   d. Teresa wants to move house but has negative equity.

30. In a transaction one of the parties is called the "mortgagee". That party is which of the following?

   a. The borrower of the mortgage loan.

   b. The person to whom the property is mortgaged.

   c. The donor of the security for the loan.

   d. The provider of the security for the loan.

31. Derek and Sonia have a joint mortgage. If, on their divorce, Derek is to retain the family home, which below will NOT be required by the lender?

   a. A property valuation for Derek's further advance request.

   b. Assignment of Sonia's life assurance policy to Derek.

   c. Sonia's written agreement to the mortgage re-arrangement.

   d. Confirmation of Derek's current financial status.

32. Vera and Jack have a joint repayment mortgage and, due to divorce, Vera wishes to be released from the mortgage. Why does this require separate approval by Samantha?

   a. Samantha and Jack are business partners.

   b. Samantha has insurable interest in Jack's life.

   c. Samantha is a guarantor of the loan.

   d. Samantha receives maintenance payments from her ex-husband Jack.

33. Tina is buying a property outright. On completion of the purchase, the property deeds are:

   a. Retained by the Land Registry.

   b. Transferred to the Land Charges Registry.

   c. Sent to Tina.

   d. Transferred to Tina's lender.

34. Commercial company applicants for a mortgage normally must provide the prospective lender with which of the following?

   a. Most recent self-assessment.
   b. Landlord's reference is to creditworthiness.
   c. Memorandum and articles of association.
   d. A guarantor offering supporting security.

35. In respect of the full endowment mortgage, which of the following statements is incorrect?

   a. Declared reversionary bonuses cannot be taken away by the insurer.
   b. The contributions receive tax relief at the contributor's highest rate.
   c. At maturity, the borrower receives a tax paid lump sum from bonuses.
   d. The sum assured is the same amount as the capital amount of the loan.

36. How is the mortgage loan usually repaid under a personal pension mortgage?

   a. From the pensioner's pension income
   b. By assignment of the pension scheme rights.
   c. From the tax-free cash lump sum available at retirement.
   d. By annual payments from the pension scheme fun

37. A guarantor agrees to:

   a. Pay the loan in full if the borrower fails to do so.
   b. Take action against the defaulting borrower.
   c. Ensure the borrower observes the loan contract.
   d. Provide a security margin if called upon to do so.

38. With regard to buildings insurance claims, a lender:

   a. Automatically receives all claims proceeds.
   b. Always has priority in directing the use of claim monies.
   c. May direct the use of claim monies.
   d. May claim any additional proceeds obtained by the borrower.

39. When completing a fact find, which one of the following can be classed as a client's liability?

   a. House.
   b. Equities.
   c. Mortgage.
   d. Personal Pension.

40. Diana is self-employed, running her own consultancy business. She has no investments or life cover. What form of protection is likely to be most suitable for her repayment mortgage in these circumstances?

   a. Personal pension term assurance
   b. Decreasing term assurance.
   c. Unit-linked endowment.
   d. With profit endowment.

41. What is the purpose of redundancy protection insurance?

   a. Provision of a lump sum in the event of redundancy.
   b. Provide monthly benefit to top up unemployment benefit.
   c. Provide monthly benefit to cover mortgage and loan repayments.
   d. Provide monthly benefit to cover normal household expenditure.

42. Under the Commonhold and Leasehold Reform Act 2002, who of the following leaseholders may have a statutory right to buy their freehold?

   a. Alison, who is 20 years into a 99-year lease on her flat.
   b. Arthur, who is 5 years into a 19-year lease on his London apartment.
   c. Roger, who 5 years ago, signed a 30-year lease on a grocery shop.
   d. Lucy, who 15 years ago, signed a 30-year lease on a warehouse.

43. £100,000 mortgage is to be repaid by a low-cost endowment policy for the same value. In what circumstances, if any, is the policy guaranteed to be sufficient to repay the mortgage?

   a. There is no guarantee.

   b. On death prior to maturity only.

   c. At the maturity date only.

   d. At the maturity date or upon death prior to maturity.

44. An adviser must take all reasonable steps to ensure that a client understands that, with a low-cost endowment mortgage

   a. The sum assured may not be sufficient to repay a mortgage on death.

   b. The policy will not have a surrender value during the first ten years.

   c. The policy has a paid-up value only during the last 10 years of the contract.

   d. The maturity value may not be sufficient to repay the mortgage.

45. Simon is buying Lucy's house. If Lucy dies between exchange of contracts and completion, what is the situation?

   a. It depends on the terms of Lucy's will.

   b. Simon may withdraw from the sale without penalty.

   c. The contract is invalid.

   d. If Simon withdraws from the sale, he will be penalised.

46. Which one of the following types of policy is the cheapest to protect a repayment mortgage in the event of the borrower's death?

   a. Level term assurance.

   b. Low-cost endowment assurance.

   c. Decreasing term assurance.

   d. Low start low-cost endowment assurance.

47. If a property is being re-mortgaged the lender:

   a. Is unlikely to require another valuation.

   b. Will probably check the borrower's status.

   c. Is unlikely to require a consent form from other adult occupants.

   d. Will probably waive administration fees.

48. Low-cost endowment mortgages are so called because:

   a. The low-cost element is achieved by capping the interest rate.

   b. The product does not normally provide reversionary bonuses.

   c. The basic sum assured is lower than that on other similar products.

   d. The basic interest rate is kept low, thus making the product cheaper.

49. Hubert wishes to sell some of the land which forms part of his mortgaged property. However, the value of the property remaining will be insufficient in relation to the mortgage. How is this likely to be dealt with?

   a. Hubert will need to increase his repayments.

   b. Hubert will need to reduce his mortgage loan.

   c. Hubert will need to purchase a mortgage indemnity guarantee policy

   d. Hubert will need to take out a second mortgage.

50. A mortgage protection policy would provide the most suitable form of protection when effected in connection with a

   a. 20-year low-cost endowment mortgage with a £2,000 mortgage cashback.

   b. 20-year repayment mortgage with interest rates fixed for the first 3 years.

   c. 25 year ISA mortgage with variable interest rates.

   d. 25-year pension mortgage with a cap and collar interest rate.

51. During the first year of a mortgage loan term, which type of interest rate option could result in the borrower paying a higher rate of interest than that prevailing?

   a. Capped and collared.
   b. Deferred interest.
   c. Discounted.
   d. Variable.

52. After she has bought her house with a mortgage, Sandra's boyfriend Sonny moved in. She has now applied for a further advance, and her lender wants to ensure that this does not allow Sonny to obtain an overriding interest in the property. How is this achieved?

   a. Sandra signs a consent to mortgage form.
   b. Sonny signs a consent to mortgage form.
   c. The Lender issues a deed of further charges.
   d. The lender issues a deed of consent.

53. Gerald was discharged from bankruptcy last year. What rule applies if Gerald now wishes to borrow?

   a. He must apply to the courts for approval.
   b. He has to wait a further two years.
   c. He must declare his previous history.
   d. He may only borrow very nominal amounts.

54. Why do early surrender values on the endowment policies used for mortgage repayment purposes appear to represent poor value?

   a. Because the large set up costs are paid for in the early years.
   b. Because returns do not start to accrue until several years into the policy
   c. Because of the high costs of providing life cover
   d. Because of the costs associated with guaranteeing mortgage repayment

55. Albert has fallen into arrears on his interest-only mortgage payments and to give himself some leeway applies to extend the term. Why is his lender unlikely to agree to this solution?

   a. His mortgage is less than five years old.
   b. His mortgage is in its final five years.
   c. He has a with-profits endowment mortgage.
   d. There is a substantial amount of loan outstanding.

56. Jane Smith and Kenneth Jones live in and own a house as joint tenants. Kenneth dies without leaving a will. What will happen to his half of the house?

    a. Its ownership will automatically be inherited by Jane.
    b. Its value will be exempt from IHT.
    c. It will be inherited by their children.
    d. It will be treated as half of his estate

57. Edward defaults on his mortgage and, following repossession, the amount owed to the lender is £6,500. If payment from a mortgage indemnity policy reduces the outstanding debt to £3,000, the insurer can sue the borrower for:

    a. £3,000.
    b. £3,500.
    c. £6,500.
    d. £9,500.

58. Each payment under a repayment mortgage loan consists of

    a. A varying amount of both capital and interest throughout the mortgage term.
    b. Interest only with the capital repayment being made separately at the end of the mortgage term.
    c. A fixed amount of both capital and interest throughout the mortgage term.
    d. Capital only with the interest due being paid separately at the end of the mortgage term.

59. The power to change mortgage interest rates:

    a. Is always subject to written notification to individual borrowers.
    b. Includes permission to change during the fixed rate period.
    c. Is contained in the legal charge.
    d. Is subject to at least seven days' notice.

60. If a client invests in a without profit endowment, what amount will be paid out at maturity or on earlier death?

    a. The sum assured
    b. The sum assured plus accrued bonuses
    c. The sum assured or the bid value of units, whichever is greater
    d. The bid value of units plus accrued bonuses.

61. Which of the following advantages is most likely to be available to borrowers under a block insurance policy provided by the lender?

   a. High-value properties covered.

   b. High quality of cover provided.

   c. Flexibility to cater for individual needs.

   d. Cover provided for range of risks.

62. Piper has a capped-rate interest-only mortgage of £150,000, with a capped rate of 5%. The lender's standard variable rate is 4% at outset. If the standard variable rate increases to 4.75% after six months and then to 5.25% three months later, what will be Piper's monthly payment of interest in month eleven?

   a. £333.33

   b. £593.75

   c. £625.00

   d. £656.25.

63. Steven took out a £40,000 interest-only mortgage loan protected by a low-cost endowment plan. At the time of his death, the endowment basic sum assured was £10,000, declared bonuses totalled £8,000, and the terminal bonus was £12,000. How much should the plan have paid out?

   a. £18,000.

   b. £30,000

   c. £40,000.

   d. £52,000.

64. Which of the following contracts cannot be used to repay an interest-only mortgage?

   a. An ISA.

   b. A convertible term assurance.

   c. An endowment.

   d. A pension.

65. Barry has a variable rate interest only mortgage. He is moving house and considering a fixed rate product. In which of the following situations might this NOT be appropriate?

   a. Indications are that interest rates are about to rise.

   b. Indications are that interest will continue to fall.

   c. Barry's budget is tight until he finishes his 3-year apprenticeship.

   d. Barry's wife intends to return to work when their 3-year-old son starts school.

66. Henry's house is currently worth £80,000. He wishes to increase his existing mortgage of £50,000 by 40%. No existing mortgage indemnity guarantee (HLC) is in place, but the lender requires one where the loan to value exceeds 85%. What HLC cover is required?

   a. £1,000.
   b. £2,000.
   c. £3,000.
   d. £4,000.

67. Because of redundancy, Shirley is in arrears on her mortgage payments. Her application for income support to help with her mortgage interest may be acceptable, providing her savings do not exceed:

   a. £4,000.
   b. £8,000.
   c. £16,000.
   d. £32,000.

68. Some borrowers like to feel that the amount they owe to the lender is being reduced by their monthly mortgage payments. They should choose a:

   a. Fixed rate mortgage.
   b. Endowment mortgage.
   c. Repayment mortgage.
   d. ISA mortgage.

69. Which one of the following statements regarding cashback mortgages is FALSE?

   a. They are particularly attractive to first-time buyers.
   b. They usually have a clawback on early redemption.
   c. A lump sum is paid once the mortgage is completed.
   d. Usually, the higher the loan to value the larger the cashback payment as the lender is lending more.

70. Why could an occupier of a property who is not the owner be asked to sign consent to mortgage form?

   a. Because that occupier would otherwise be precluded from residence by the mortgage deed.

   b. Because the lender wishes to ensure that the occupier also becomes responsible for the loan.

   c. Because the lender wants to ensure that the property's building insurance remains valid.

   d. Because that occupier's rights might adversely affect the lender's right to possession.

71. Stuart has taken out a mortgage with a rate 'discount' of 2% for the first 3 years. This means:

   a. The initial discount is added to the outstanding capital.

   b. The 2% reduction will be clawed back at the end of 3 years.

   c. There will be no restrictions on how soon Stuart can repay the mortgage

   d. There is likely to be a penalty if Stuart repays the mortgage during this period.

72. Oscar has recently been asked to complete a "consent to mortgage" form. Because he is:

   a. acting as guarantor for a friend's mortgage application

   b. Moving into his girlfriend's mortgaged house as she applies for a further advance.

   c. Being released from a joint mortgage contract following divorce.

   d. Selling a portion of his large garden to a property developer.

73. Under the right-to-buy legislation in England, after what period, if any, can the owner usually sell the property without penalty?

   a. 18 months.

   b. 3 years.

   c. 5 years.

   d. There is always a penalty.

74. Under which of the following circumstances is an equitable interest created?

   a. Susan gives her holiday home to her sister.

   b. Susan and her sister jointly buy a holiday home using a joint mortgage.

   c. Susan formally sells a share in her holiday home to her sister.

   d. Susan lends money to her sister to buy a holiday home but retains the deeds as security.

75. Under the Commonhold and Leasehold Reform, Act 2002, the borrower has the right to:

   a. Enfranchisement in a flat development with 35% commercial usage.

   b. Buy the freehold in a flat development with 15% commercial usage.

   c. Set the price at which the freehold may be purchased.

   d. Insist on a lease extension of 100 years.

76. Which of the following alterations is LEAST likely to require Local Authority or Town Planning consent?

   a. Closing in a porch.

   b. Converting a loft.

   c. Extending a kitchen.

   d. Adding a second garage.

77. Consolidation is:

   a. The right to refuse redemption of one mortgage without the other being redeemed.

   b. The right of a lender to combine two or more loans, made by that lender to a person.

   c. The duty of the lender to advance additional monies where the deed so provides.

   d. Where a lender makes a further advance and takes priority over an earlier loan by another.

78. Rita's building society insisted that the plan supporting her proposed mortgage must be assigned to them. Which of the following would NOT be appropriate?

   a. A with-profits endowment from a friendly society.

   b. A unit-linked whole of life from a bancassurer.

   c. A decreasing term assurance from a mutual insurance company.

   d. A Personal pension from a proprietary insurance company.

79. Robin is significantly in arrears with his mortgage payments, and the County Court has granted his lender all outright possession order. This is likely to the lender to take possession:

   a. With immediate effect.

   b. On the following working day.

   c. Within 7 days.

   d. Within 28 days.

80. Which of the following statements is correct in regard to mortgage indemnity insurances (HLC s)?

   a. HLCs cover the borrower against his inability to repay the loan.

   b. HLCs cover the lender against the borrower's inability to repay.

   c. HLCs insure against the borrower's death before full repayment.

   d. HLCs will not insure against any more than 75% of any one loss.

81. How much stamp duty will be charged on a house bought for £350,000 in August 2019 for a second-time purchaser?

   a. £3,600.

   b. £4,500.

   c. £7,500.

   d. £10,500.

CeMAP 2 Specimen Exam

82. Fred and Mavis are married. Fred is the registered owner of the house they live in. Fred wishes to raise a loan on the house. Which of the following will the lender require of Mavis?

    a. She to agree to join in as a joint borrower.

    b. She to give a waiver of rights of residence.

    c. She to waive rights to a share of the property.

    d. She to act as the loan guarantor as she is resident.

83. Tom is about to effect an equity release arrangement. Which of the following features indicate that it is a home reversion scheme as opposed to a home income scheme?

    a. The loan will be repaid on death.

    b. Tax relief is exceptionally still available.

    c. A percentage of the property will be sold.

    d. The scheme will be set up on a joint life basis.

84. Which of the following is NOT likely to be included in an APR calculation?

    a. Lender's legal fees.

    b. Daily interest rate.

    c. Borrower's solicitor's fees.

    d. Mortgagee's administration charges.

85. A solicitor wishes to check that the street in which his client's prospective house is located, is not subject to a town planning scheme. Which is the appropriate search for him to carry out?

    a. Land Registry Search.

    b. Land Charges Registry Search.

    c. Local Land Charges Search.

    d. Commons Registration Search.

86. The lender, when selling a repossessed property, has an obligation to

    a. Keep the property on the market until contracts are exchanged.

    b. Achieve the valuation price of the property.

    c. Pay the surplus funds into court.

    d. Pay a proportion of the proceeds to the CML Repossessions Registry.

87. Ian has entered into an arrangement with his mortgage lender. This means he has:

   a. Taken out a new first mortgage.

   b. Received approval for a second mortgage.

   c. Reduced his mortgage term.

   d. Agreed the term over which to repay arrears.

88. A specialised mortgage house:

   a. Lends on a centralised basis and is mainly funded from the wholesale market.

   b. Lends on a decentralised basis and is mainly funded from the wholesale market.

   c. Lends on a centralised basis and is mainly funded from the retail market.

   d. Lends on a decentralised basis and is mainly funded from the retail market.

89. A plot of land, with outline planning permission to build a house, has been sold to a builder. What action (if any) need be taken in order for the erection of a house to be sanctioned by the local authority?

   a. No action is required of the builder.

   b. An undertaking and a site guarantee must be given.

   c. A copy of the building plans needs to be submitted for information only.

   d. Planning consent needs to be applied for.

90. Which is the highest risk method of repaying a mortgage?

   a. Interest only and a Personal pension

   b. Interest only and unit trust ISA

   c. Interest only and a with-profits Personal pension

   d. Interest only and with profits low-cost endowment

91. Kate is looking for a single repayment vehicle for her interest only mortgage. What factor ruled out a ISA mortgage in favour of a low-cost endowment mortgage?

   a. The loan is in single, not joint names.

   b. She required a higher than anticipated size of loan.

   c. She was a higher rate taxpayer.

   d. Her state of health was poor.

92. Personal drawings by a self-employed person applying for a mortgage:
   a. May give an inaccurate indication of income.
   b. Must not exceed net profit for a given year.
   c. Are averaged over a three year period.
   d. Are disregarded if the business is less than five years old.

93. Mandy and Mark wish to make their own arrangements for buildings and contents insurance. Which of the following conditions is LEAST likely to apply?
   a. Mandy and Mark must notify the lender if they intend to lapse the policy.
   b. The cover arranged must meet with the approval of the lender.
   c. The lender will be entitled to commission on the cover arranged.
   d. The lender may have control over the money should Mandy and Mark make the claim.

94. When there is a joint life first death low-cost endowment policy assigned to a lender and one of the borrowers dies during the mortgage term, who initially receives the policy proceeds?
   a. The deceased's estate.
   b. The borrower's solicitor.
   c. The surviving borrower.
   d. The lender.

95. Amy has a Personal pension linked mortgage, and Ron has an ISA mortgage. This means that
   a. Ron's underlying investment vehicle can be written in joint names.
   b. Amy's mortgage is guaranteed to be fully repaid at the end of the term.
   c. Ron's investment plan is free of all capital gains tax.
   d. Amy's net mortgage interest costs will be affected by her tax status.

96. Assuming that agreed regular payments are maintained, which type of mortgage always guarantees to have repaid the mortgage loan at the end of the term?

    a. A capital and interest mortgage.

    b. An ISA-linked mortgage.

    c. A low-cost endowment-linked mortgage.

    d. A pension-linked mortgage.

97. Under what circumstances would a court set aside a redemption clause in the terms and conditions of a mortgage?

    a. If it considers that it is there to deliberately prevent repayment.

    b. If it considers that the terms of the clause are complex.

    c. If the clause was not shown prominently in the terms and conditions.

    d. If the borrower's attention was not specifically drawn to this clause prior to completion

98. It is a legal requirement that lenders quote an APR when:

    a. Advertising a mortgage service.

    b. Advertising a mortgage rate.

    c. Sending out annual mortgage statements.

    d. Sending out redemption quotations.

99. Lenders generally include a condition in their mortgage deeds which says that the lender by making the loan is not saying the price of the property is correct. Why is this so?

    a. To ensure the guarantor is fully aware of the guaranteed liability.

    b. To ensure the borrower does not make a claim against the lender.

    c. To allow the lender to decline to make any additional advances.

    d. To ensure the mortgage indemnity policy issuer is aware of the risk.

100. Why is an open bridging facility said to be a high risk?

   a. Because the desired alternative property may not be worth the price.

   b. Because the borrower has not yet obtained a buyer for his property.

   c. Because the existing property may be overpriced in the market.

   d. Because the new property may be encumbered with onerous covenants.

Answers

1. D	26. C	51. A	76. A
2. B	27. C	52. B	77. B
3. A	28. B	53. C	78. D
4. C	29. B	54. A	79. D
5. D	30. D	55. C	80. B
6. C	31. B	56. A	81. C
7. C	32. C	57. B	82. B
8. C	33. C	58. A	83. C
9. A	34. C	59. C	84. C
10. A	35. B	60. A	85. C
11. D	36. C	61. B	86. C
12. B	37. A	62. C	87. D
13. B	38. C	63. C	88. A
14. B	39. C	64. B	89. D
15. C	40. B	65. B	90. B
16. B	41. C	66. B	91. B
17. B	42. A	67. C	92. A
18. C	43. B	68. C	93. C
19. C	44. D	69. D	94. D
20. B	45. D	70. D	95. C
21. A	46. C	71. D	96. A
22. A	47. B	72. B	97. A
23. D	48. C	73. C	98. B
24. C	49. B	74. D	99. B
25. A	50. B	75. B	100. B

Printed in Great Britain
by Amazon